The Thought Coach

by

Geoff Hart

Grosvenor House
Publishing Limited

This book is published by
Grosvenor House Publishing Ltd
28-30 High Street, Guildford, Surrey, GU1 3EL.
www.grosvenorhousepublishing.co.uk

A CIP record for this book
is available from the British Library

ISBN 978-1-78148-565-1

*This book is dedicated to four very special ladies, who
collectively have been inspiring, guiding
and motivating me throughout my life.*

*My dear 84 years young Mum, Josie.
My darling wife and soul mate Lin,
and our two beautiful daughters Sheryl and Nicola.
With all my love and thanks.*

CONTENTS

CONTENTS

CONTENTS

INTRODUCTION

QUALITY THINKING

We are all great thinkers.

We think about this, that and everything in between. We love happy thoughts, but sometimes they are anything but. Like them or not, we live our lives as a direct result of our thoughts and in turn our thinking has a direct link to all our feelings.

What's on your mind right now?

From the moment we wake up, every second is absorbed with our conscious thoughts. Even when we are asleep, our unconscious mind is busy working away creating our dreams as well as ensuring we continue to breath the oxygen required to keep us alive.

With all this going on, is it any wonder that life can get on top of us. Making us feel stressed or anxious, becoming overloaded and frustrated, and for some, feeling totally out of control. If any of these descriptions sound familiar, you are not alone.

To some degree or another, most of us collect baggage on our journey through life. We worry about different life issues, especially those that seem to be controlling us, whilst for others success always seems out of reach, or difficult to maintain.

Whatever your situation, The Thought Coach will pinpoint and guide you to the answers that will help improve your quality of life, if you let it. Let me explain why.

The more books I have read and the more research I've carried out, the one and only thing I have found that has a total and lasting impact on a fulfilled, content, happy and enjoyable life starts and finishes with our thinking and the thoughts that we are carrying around with us every moment of every day. Neither have I ever met or read about a single person who has led a totally worthwhile, fulfilled, complete and successful life without needing help, support, guidance and knowledge from others.

In this book, together we will explore different avenues that can start to make more, or better sense of your life and also learn how to confidently tackle the challenges and behaviours that often stop us from moving forward.

The fact that you have started reading this book is a signal that something in your life may be missing, out of alignment, or quite simply you know it could be better, more fulfilling, more fun.

The Thought Coach is filled with actions and strategies that will have a real and positive impact on the life you lead. Starting RIGHT NOW, I will help move you from where you are currently, to where you want to be. In just

60 minutes you will start to see that you can take better control of your life and make it more enjoyable.

With each chapter you read and each action undertaken, you will notice positive changes starting to take place. You'll become more confident in yourself, more understanding of others, more self-assured, more aware, and motivated to bring out the very best in every aspect of your life.

We all have opportunities to enjoy our life, with the same number of hours each day in which to do it. It's how we use our time and the quality of our thinking, that gives us and shapes our identity. What hasn't worked in the past, be it yesterday or last year is gone, it's behind us now.

All the future that will unfold before us is new, untouched, compelling, exciting. There can be no regrets of the future, only lessons of the past. You are in charge of your own destiny!

Sounds great doesn't it? So let's get started on this exciting new journey together!

Start wherever you like! This may be chapter one, or looking at the contents list, you may be drawn to start elsewhere. It doesn't matter, this is your book and you get to set the agenda. Each chapter has its own helpful strategies, actions and exercises. Pick it up and put it down when you want, but keep it close to hand! If an exercise feels right, do it! If not, come back to it another time. The more of the book you read, the more different perspectives of your thinking you will be able to discover and control. Remember, our thoughts have a direct link to our feelings. This book will guide and then show you how to move your emotions quickly and successfully to a better state.

From anger........... to calm
From unsure................to confident
And from frustrated .... to fulfilled

UNDER YOUR BONNET...BRAIN POWER

Our brains are unique, have amazing abilities and fantastic potential. They are the control centre of our body, process our thoughts, control our temperature, breathing, learning, emotions and so much more.

Just like a computer, our brain runs its own software and houses a vast communication centre, sending and receiving messages 24/7. Incredibly complex, our brain is also home to our most precious memories, hopes and aspirations for the future.

It contains cells called neurons, which are the building blocks of our nervous system, housing an estimated 100 billion of them, which in nanoseconds can transmit information throughout the body.

Each neuron forms connections with between a thousand and twenty thousand other neurons, resulting in trillions of minute connections. Research tells us this is more than all the stars in all the galaxies of the universe and this brain activity creates sufficient electricity to power a light bulb.

With all this incredible hardware at our personal disposal and the energy it creates, we already have the capacity to achieve as much as we choose to in our lives.

Yes, we really have, because by internally reprogramming, we can change unwanted or negative, destructive behaviours, replacing them with new empowering ones that could serve us better on our journey through life, as well as improve the quality of our thinking. To explain how, it's useful to understand more about our thoughts.

We have our conscious, surface structure thoughts, which we use all the time, to make choices, to plan, calculate, and to communicate. You are reading this at a conscious level. Then there are our unconscious, deeper structure thoughts, sometimes referred to as subconscious thinking. This is where real life changing breakthroughs can take place, as well as effective learning, in a totally holistic way.

How?

Our unconscious mind has absorbed and stored everything we have ever learnt in our lifetime, it accepts everything and cannot differentiate between perceived or real. Positive, negative, good and bad, useful or destructive. It builds beliefs from all the data it has been passed from the conscious mind then stores it until needed, as we move along life's journey.

By understanding how to identify the beliefs that may be holding us back or are no longer useful to us, from the ones that can help us achieve the quality we want from our lives, we can accomplish fast, effective, positive and lasting results. We will explore this further in the chapter on Values and Beliefs.

Our mind and our thoughts are associated with the largest part of the brain called the cerebrum, which in turn is divided into two parts, known as the left and right hemispheres. The left hemisphere is more analytical and performs all the processes involved in thinking, communicating, judging, planning and organising. The right hemisphere is creative and colourful, more abstract. We use this side for music, colour and shapes.

As you will discover in more detail in the chapter on Visualisation, we think in pictures, yet so many people find themselves unable to harness and utilise this right side as often or as fully as it could be.

For this reason, I will teach you strategies that will bring out your creative and natural talent. Being able to utilise both sides of your brain will open up more possibilities for you in today's fast moving world, offer more opportunities, allowing you to think differently and more effectively in all aspects of your life.

As I have mentioned, our minds have the ability to be guided into areas that can help move our lives forward and away from thoughts that have held us back. By changing old and unhelpful internal software programmes, we can change any unwanted behaviours. Much of this work is done on an unconscious level, by preventing our surface level and conscious (often limiting) thoughts from blocking positive and long lasting changes.

A good analogy is de-cluttering. Many people have found it liberating to de-clutter their home, a room or space that has lost its purpose. Sorting out things that are no longer used or have served their purpose, placed in piles, perhaps one for a local boot fair or charity, then maybe a trip to the local tip with broken items.

Those I have spoken to tell me that going through this process brings real and exciting clarity. When actioned, it creates a new energy, gives motivation, purpose, hope, a new and fresh beginning. This in turn opens up all sorts of new possibilities, a new blank canvas to work with, even create your own masterpiece.

With clear and open space, this new environment brings fresh promise, a more relaxed state, an opportunity to be inspired, creative, perhaps even redesign or redecorate. Yet all so often we fail to do the same with our own life. We keep clutter (old or obsolete brain software) that is holding us back or remain weighed down by the burden of past regrets and mistakes. Issues that could be resolved in minutes are left for days, weeks and sometimes a lifetime, stopping us giving of our best, and more importantly stopping us from living the full, happy and content life we seek.

None of us would buy a car and run it year after year without a service or oil change and expect it to go on running smoothly. Our brains are working constantly. Researchers tell us we each have a staggering 21 million thoughts a year, that's an average of 60,000 thoughts each and every day. Yet how many of us regularly feed our brains, train our brains, or until now be aware that we could improve or change unhelpful obsolete software?

The great news is that by utilising the models and strategies contained within The Thought Coach, you can improve the software in your brain. You can remove unhelpful, unwanted thoughts, disabling beliefs and behaviours, replacing them with constructive, inspired and positive thinking.

You are unique. You have a purpose and with these techniques to improve and enhance your brain power, you can design a compelling, more rewarding future, bringing quality, inner peace and happiness to the next chapters of your life.

CHAPTER 1

UNDERSTANDING YOURSELF

Before we try to make sense of why others do things that we find annoying, upsetting or even downright dangerous, it is useful to first take a step back and understand ourselves a little better.

OUR MAP OF THE WORLD

The way in which we try to make sense of what is going on in our heads is supported by something called our internal representational system, a system based upon our five senses through which we use to remember the past, assess the present and imagine the future.

Through our internal representational system we take in all the hundreds of thousands of pieces of information we are bombarded with every waking second; our experiences are mapped, sorted and filtered into manageable chunks so that it can be represented in a way that is uniquely meaningful to us. Although the system of sorting and filtering is common to us all; each individual has a unique way of using it – thus we all have our own unique map of the world.

We all have our own map of the world...

What we see, what we hear and what we feel, all help make up our world, as well as language, decisions, memories, beliefs that we hold and our personal values, the things that we stand for and won't compromise over.

Let me give you an example of what I mean by the way we absorb and filter information. Have you ever had two people telling you about the same event, it may also have been an event you went to. From the way they were both describing it, you felt like they were talking about two totally different events, two different occasions.

That is why, when you see people being asked what they thought about a show, concert or event they have attended, they may talk so differently about their experience. You too may even have a different view as you reflect on the same occasion than them.

The reason for this is as our representational system absorbed all the sounds, sights and emotions of the event, we, for want of a better phrase, "put our own spin on it". Consequently, a piece of information that was important or even critical for one person was irrelevant to another.

One person may tell the story by generalising, missing out much of the content of the event, whilst another may talk about the great atmosphere, whilst others may focus on a totally different part of it, maybe the sounds, or for another the smells. Someone else may highlight the visual spectacle of the event, or another person distort the information. In other words, each and every one of us has our own map of the world.

Another great example is captured brilliantly in the recent movie, adapted from the book "The Best Exotic Marigold Hotel". In essence, a group of Brits from different backgrounds all end up staying at the same hotel in India. Through their unique maps of the world, you get a different perspective of India. For some it's an adventure, loving the bright colours and soaking up all the many aromas and sights to treasure. Whilst for another member in the group, it is a total nightmare, full of noise, cramped, with people rushing everywhere, hustle, bustle and car fume smelly.

So why is it useful for you to know this? Quite simply because our map of the world has a direct effect on our emotional state and physiology. By changing our internal filters we can change our experience of the world. It can also give us great insight into others and how we may misunderstand them. All because their map of the world is different to ours. What is obvious to them is not to us and vice versa, our perspectives being different.

The more flexible we try to be, the more at ease we become with ourselves. Do you recall a time when you just had to make your point, you were right, they were wrong, you weren't going to step down or back away. Well neither was the other person! The end result being both parties feeling miserable and down.

How did it make you feel? For many it leads to sleepless nights, a result of going to bed angry. In its worst form, it's the sort of stalemate that can bring about a breakdown in a relationship and cause any number of illnesses.

Could you be more flexible next time? Try looking at it from a different perspective. Being able to let it go or bring closure more quickly, is not a sign of weakness, it's a sign of strength and doesn't have to compromise your values either.

There is a helpful exercise on perceptual positions in the Values and Beliefs chapter.

MODALITY BUILDING BLOCKS

Another key part of our representational system is called modalities. Our modalities are the building blocks of our experiences. They allow us to fine tune things internally by using what is known as our sub-modalities.

All our experiences are coded in our unconscious and just like our map of the world we distort, delete, filter out and generalise information. These all influence our feelings and consequently our emotions. So what one person might feel as a painful experience may not affect another in the same way.

With our modalities we have three main areas that we predominantly use and each of us favours one more than the others when storing and filtering information:

Visual - what we see

Auditory - what we hear (including self-talk)

Kinaesthetic – the physical feelings associated with what we see and hear

In addition, our other senses are smell and taste (olfactory and gustatory).

Each of these modalities has a vast range of sub-modalities to it. To explain further, imagine the control room of a recording studio with all its buttons, dials and sliders. You are the producer and depending on which way you turn the dial or push the slider, you can go from really quiet, to a comfortable sound, to very loud. When you start to press each button you control its expanse and you can do exactly the same with each one of your senses.

Hence you can also internally tune the visual. Hold an image in your mind. Is it bright or dark, can you add colour, is it moving or still? Is it crystal clear and close up or some way off in the distance?

With your physical feeling (kinaesthetic) sub-modalities, what is the quality of the sensations that are there? Warm, cool, cold, hard or soft, rough or smooth? Where is the feeling located in your body, how intense is the feeling? Just spend a few moments thinking about these questions, then remember a time perhaps when you felt anxious in the past and you got a particular feeling. Was it located in the pit of your stomach or did it make you feel sick, dizzy or light headed? Did it tighten across your chest or affect your breathing? Starting to understand where these various feelings are located in your body is key to bringing positive change for the future.

By being able to change these sub-modalities, many people have quickly overcome phobias, unwanted habits and behaviours without the need of long term therapy simply by changing the internal representation and therefore the experience associated with it, as well as making happy and pleasurable events even happier and more memorable.

Have a go now and start to think about any one of your senses. Think about something you really enjoyed, something special that has happened for you and begin to remember as if it were happening now. Turn up the sub-modality of that sense a little more, make it brighter, louder or feel even better. Now close your eyes, take a deep breath and relive that moment, before moving on, turning the sub-modality up a little then down a little. Notice the subtle differences and experience how valuable this inner power will be as you move forward in your life.

Having the resources to associate into (re-experience) or dissociate (observe without re-experiencing) a memory can give you a new freedom, a new control. There is a technique on this later in the chapter.

LIVING WITH OTHERS

At the time of writing this, according to the U.S. census bureau on the world population there are over 7 billion of us, increasing to around 8 billion over the next 30 years.

The U.K. population has over 63 million, so pretty much wherever we live we are in contact with people and throughout our lifetime we are likely to meet thousands of others.

The better equipped we are at dealing with relationships, the better we understand others and where they are coming from, the more comfortable our own lives will be.

What is the synergy, the chemistry that brings people together, to enjoy each other's company, so much so that they become friends, sometimes for life, sometimes soul mates.....Rapport.

RAPPORT

When we talk to someone with ease and are on the same wavelength, we are in rapport. For some reason we can get on with others whom we have only just met, as if we have been friends for years.

In a crowded room or coffee house, look around and you will notice two people so absorbed in a conversation with each other, that they are oblivious to what else is happening.

Another example is to watch a frustrated customer with faulty goods in a shop talking to an assistant and how the body language and expressions, or even raised voices show how out of rapport they are.

This starts to explain both how useful understanding rapport is and why developing skills to gain rapport with others quickly can be invaluable. Good salesman and customer service teams learn how to use rapport and build relationships with potential clients as quickly as possible. Most of us however encounter situations within our own circle of friends, family and working environment, as well as the one I have highlighted within the shop, where better skills could prevent us from walking away angry, upset, or misunderstood, where better rapport and interpersonal skills could have helped.

Rapport can bring about a different result, a better result for both us and the person we are talking to, as well as create trust. The first place to start is to accept people's own perspective on life, don't judge them, or their values. Simply acknowledge they have a different map of the world to us. As we start to communicate with others also understand that,

"YOU CANNOT NOT COMMUNICATE".

Take a moment to think about what this means. Whether we say something out loud or say nothing we are still communicating. People do not communicate with language alone. In fact, only 7% of what we communicate is the words we use. 38% is verbal behaviour and 55% is non-verbal behaviour or body language. So it's not what you say sometimes, it's what you don't say that others will hear, pick up on and interpret through their unique map of the world.

There are a number of ways in which we communicate totally independently of speech, some of which I list below:

Skin colour/tones
Breathing rate
Body language and movement
Posture
Eye contact and movement
Voice/pitch/tone/volume/rhythm/speed
Facial expressions
Gestures/arm/hands/legs/feet

As well as the words/language we use when we communicate, we have a preference as to what we say, how we say it, the expressions we use, how we stand or sit.

Whilst body language is a vast subject in its own right, with better understanding you can improve your rapport with others fast, simply by observing some of these areas and then matching the person and their preference. Listen to the words being used, remember that within their language pattern, they will be using words reflecting their own preferences, their own map of the world. To help increase rapport, introduce some of the same words they use as you speak to them.

Look at their physiology and adopt a similar match. If they speak in a soft tone, speak more gently. This flexibility will be useful in building relationships, as well as taking the fire out of an angry confrontation. Mirroring gently the movements of the other person can also improve rapport as well as matching them. This is not mimicking them or making fun, it's purely a way of you getting the most from the conversation or relationship and building great rapport.

A final point on communicating with others is that our intention and our impact may be two totally different things.

We judge ourselves on our intention...
Others judge us on our impact.

ASSOCIATION DISSOCIATION TECHNIQUE

If you want to change a bad experience or memory or enhance a happy memory, the following technique will help by utilising your sub-modalities control.

Sit in a quiet place where you won't be distracted and begin by taking long deep breaths and start to feel yourself relax. In the calm of the moment, begin by thinking about two memories from your past. Firstly, notice a pleasant and happy memory. Notice if you are re-experiencing it in an associated way, from behind your own eyes, seeing what you saw through your own eyes again, hearing what you heard through your own ears again and feeling what you felt in your own body, what you felt then, as if you were actually there again.

Or are you observing this pleasant or happy memory in a dissociated way, as if you were watching yourself do something in a film?

If you associated with the good memory, take time to notice the modalities, and sub-modalities (qualities) linked with the experience. What do you see, is it close or far away? Can you make the picture bigger and brighter? Try to move the colours down, then bring them back again, this time even clearer, richer and more vibrant. Now hear what's going on around as you are in this happy memory. Is it noisy or quiet, what's the pitch, is it all around you? Try to turn the volume up, then down.

Did anything change internally when you did this? What have you become more aware of?

By associating with the good memory, you are part of the story and it's a happy place to be. Even so, you now see that by adjusting your sub-modalities you can enhance the experience and make it even better.

With this pleasant memory what feelings does it give you? Where are they located, where do they start? You can spin all these good feelings around your entire body. Where are they moving to and where does the feeling become more intense?

For the second part of this exercise choose an annoying or mildly unpleasant memory, but not one that's too traumatic or upsetting. Notice how you recall it. Are you associating with the experience, being in it, reliving it or dissociating yourself from it, as if watching on a TV?

Next, picture yourself sitting in your seat and watching yourself on a screen. Watch the memory from there, as you become dissociated, or even more dissociated from the memory, notice how your feelings change. Notice what you notice.

When you have a bad or unpleasant memory, you can use your sub-modalities to dissociate or detach yourself from it, make it further away and if it's in colour, go ahead and fade it. Each change can help to take away some of the painful experience or memory.

If you associated with this unpleasant memory, you have the ability to make the internal changes and dissociate yourself from it, by following this technique even further.

Begin by thinking about the unpleasant memory and as you notice what you notice, step out of the picture and stand behind what's going on as if you are there but watching as an observer, rather than being in it. Now picture that you are in a cinema. You are stepping back again, so you're now watching you, watching you on the screen. The more you dissociate from the memory, the less painful to watch it becomes.

Now with all you have learned from your sub-modalities, start to change the movie. Make the picture dimmer. If it's in colour, what happens if you make it black and white? Go ahead and try!

If it's loud, do you want to turn the volume down or even make it silent? Go ahead, you are in total control of making all the changes you want to make, to dissociate from this memory. If you want to, you could even blink and make the screen become a pinprick, then disappear. Whatever internal changes you made to bring about positive change, you will now only have the feelings of a detached observer.

❖ FOOD FOR THOUGHT ❖

1. We all have our own map of the world and filter information from our internal representational system.
2. By changing our filters we can change our emotional state, moving us to a better place when needed.
3. Our sub-modalities allow us to fine-tune our internal representational system and therefore change or erase a bad experience or phobia.
4. Good rapport and flexibility can improve our relationship with others.
5. You cannot not communicate.
6. The Association Dissociation technique allows you to change a bad experience or enhance a happy memory.

CHAPTER 2

VALUES AND BELIEFS

Our values dictate how we live our lives, how we interact with others, as well as the strategies we use along life's journey. When we are aligned with our values, they can provide stimulation, motivation, clarity and peace of mind. In essence, values are "what we value", they clarify who we are and what makes us unique. Our core values are things we do not like to compromise.

Values are at the very heart of our being and can be evidenced by the way we behave and by what we say. It is our values that make us take action. We become very uncomfortable if we find we are forced to take action that conflicts with our core values.

You may value your health or freedom, others may value things like success, adventure, excitement, power, clarity, honesty, perfection, a sense of belonging or total isolation. Some might value creativity or peace, wealth, faith or structure.

Those who value friendship or value family, may well see some or all of the following included in their list of values:

Loving
Caring
Helpful
Loyal
Friendship

PERSONAL VALUES

What is it that you value?

A great exercise, even for those of you that may have done this in the past, is to spend some time thinking about, then noting down values that are part of you. This new insight or heightened awareness will start to help you understand yourself and also others better.

What makes you the unique and special person you are?

Start with, "I value...", then jot down everything that comes to mind. As your list grows, look over it and highlight or draw circles around the ones that really stand out for you. Ones that are at the heart of your being.

There are likely to be around five values that you will not be prepared to compromise for anyone or any thing. These are your core values and may even give an insight or clues into your mission in life, in effect your purpose. What you do with your time, what you want to achieve on a personal level to give you a satisfying and meaningful life.

Many companies have mission statements and values. These give an insight into what they do and what they stand for, as well as a benchmark to which employees are expected to work, which unfortunately at times becomes the cause of both internal and external conflicts. Sometimes corporate values may not be in alignment with your own and you may be asked to do tasks which conflict with your values, in effect having to go against what you stand for.

In other cases, some companies' stated values are only used for marketing purposes and only when it suits them. This again can create issues for those recruited into companies who adhere to the same true values. That said, the majority of companies use values as a way of being transparent and by sharing values, giving a positive benchmark for every employee from director to apprentice. Using values in this way can create a great synergy within an organisation.

As I have highlighted in chapter one, something we need to be aware of is that if we all have a different set of values, we will be different, with our different maps of the world. We cannot force our values onto others, they are ours. Before charging in and judging others, why not try to be more flexible? It will take patience and practice but allow yourself to see the other person's view of their world and with perspective thinking, view through their eyes.

An exercise on perspective thinking, is often referred to as:

"PERCEPTUAL POSITIONS"

Start by placing three chairs in a room, although this can also be carried out by standing in three different spaces.

Sit in the first chair and talk through an issue, conflict or challenge that you may currently have from your own perspective. Describe how you see it and your thoughts on the subject. (This is known as the first position perspective and is an associated experience).

Now physically stand up, turn around and shake out the experience from your body and distract your mind from this perspective. For instance, you could think of what you had for breakfast. This is known as "break state", thinking of something totally different.

Now choose another chair or place in the room and take the second position. This is the position of the other person, the way they see it, the spin they have put on the issue. Try to be the other person, sit like them, use the language they use, imagine what they might feel and try to feel it too. How does this person (not you) perceive the situation from their perspective? (This is also an associated experience).

As before, break state again. Physically shake out the experience from your body and distract your mind away from this perspective. Before continuing, make sure you have dissociated from both previous experiences fully. For example, you could ask yourself, "What's the weather doing today?"

Now move to the third chair or position. This is the position of a detached observer, someone who has been listening to both sides of the story, someone who without judging either side can give feedback on what was said and also identify some common ground. Listen carefully to what they are saying to you, thanking them for their input.

By taking perceptual positions, you will be given greater insight, greater clarity.

This new, more adaptable thinking will always lead to a better understanding. In addition, you will often find that this extra flexibility leads to sufficient common ground for you to achieve a resolution without your values being compromised. All because you have changed your own perspective and therefore approach, fully appreciating the other person's perspective. This new understanding will be transmitted in your communication and the other person's behaviour will be different as a consequence. The difficult person seems not so difficult after all, now that you are able to be more flexible.

It is not though always about accepting the unsociable behaviour of others or even putting up with unprincipled employers. It's about being flexible enough in your own world, not to let it detrimentally affect you or your values.

How can you use your values to guide your behaviour?

Your feelings are directly linked to your emotions, so you will know almost instantly when you are starting to conflict with your values. For example, if honesty is a core value and you're given the wrong change in a shop, say

£10 too much, you would start to feel uncomfortable and take action to give the money back. Whereas others with a different set of values may pocket the mistake, without a second thought.

BELIEFS

Beliefs are the rules we live by. They are very real to us. We believe them to be true. Some are in fact true, however many are not, BUT WE STILL BELIEVE THEM!

Our beliefs are collected along life's journey from a number of sources. Facts and logic through to intuition, science, personal experience and our own emotional convictions. They are all stored in our subconscious, which controls the hormones within us. In effect, they can influence the physical behaviour of all parts of our body.

When we start to separate the true beliefs from the ones that we harbour in our minds that have absolutely no substance or foundation in fact, we can start to move forward and stop limiting our potential. Limiting beliefs do just that, they stop us in our tracks and stop us living our lives to the full.

The power of belief is incredible, if we harness it positively we can achieve great things in our lives. I will expand on pre-suppositions later in the book, but evidence confirms that positive pre-suppositions can deliver many helpful life strategies.

As I say, belief is incredibly powerful. People who without any substance believe they are ill....can become ill. Likewise, positive unwavering belief has cured many illnesses, including cancer.

Research has shown time and time again that the placebo effect, along with a strong belief or faith can improve health and cure illness, all because the patient believed in the tablet they were taking, even though there were no drugs contained within it. A Swiss surgeon Theodor Kocker was able to carry out some 1,600 operations in the 1890's without giving anaesthetic. Belief is so powerful it can deliver unwavering results, as the following stories illustrate.

During 2010 many of us witnessed miracles following the tragic earthquake in Haiti. I remember watching the news some three days after the tremors had destroyed and flattened homes and lives, yet through all the carnage and rubble we witnessed a survivor being pulled out. I quickly grabbed my pen, as I heard them talk through a translator to the media and said, "I never thought I was going to die". Once again proof that our thoughts can become our reality.

There was no further good news from Haiti for another 5 long days, then suddenly a woman was brought out alive from under the bank where she worked. She had survived for 8 days. "I always believed I would be found alive", Ginette Sinport told the rescue team. Incidentally, so did her husband, who had visited the bank every day since the quake, believing she would be found alive and so it was!

This event was later followed by the news that 27 miners in Chile had been trapped. One rescue attempt followed another. It was 17 days into the search when it was confirmed that not only were the miners all still alive, they had been coping brilliantly. They had positive thoughts and positive beliefs they would be rescued. One attempt followed another to bore a hole big enough to bring them to the surface. The rest is history, history showing that belief had won the day. Belief of the miners, belief of their families and belief of the rescuers.

Then there is the story of Malcolm, well into his seventies. He was diagnosed with prostate cancer and in his own words told me, "The specialists told me there was no hope, but I didn't believe them". Malcolm had a wife, family and grandchildren, a determination to live and a strong belief that he would overcome his illness. Malcolm firmly believes that what goes on upstairs, as he calls it, what we think about, plays out in our lives. Eight years on, Malcolm is still living life to the full. I met him at the gym just this very morning, going for his workout.

As you sit here reading this you might believe I can't cook a brilliant meal or I'm not artistic or creative, so I can't paint a picture, or I can't speak in front of a group because I'm not confident or I can't take up this sport because I'm not fit enough, or I can't build a great business.

Very few of us ever live to our true potential because we don't think we can, so we don't even try. We are in control of our thoughts and what we choose, or not choose to believe.

Notice the only difference between can and can't is the T, so save that for drinking!

Many of us have owned or drive today a motor car built by giant manufacturer Ford. Its founder, Henry Ford, in early years of development of his numerous prototypes and cars famously said, "If you believe you can, or believe you can't, ...you're right". To me, the brilliance of this man and his quote sums up so much about us, what we believe and the way we think.

You may have been told at school that you can't draw or someone once said you're not any good at this or that. You may then have spent all the years since believing them and not letting the belief go, even though it's total bull. You believed in Father Christmas as a youngster and had no trouble letting go as you realised it wasn't true.

It's time to move on, look forward, discover and release the more amazing and powerful you, with all your true potential. It's time to stop being restricted by old unreal beliefs. If you change the way you think, it will change the way you feel and subsequently the way you behave.

The exercise below will allow you to,

"CREATE A BRIGHTER FUTURE",

with new empowering beliefs and the ability to leave all those old limiting beliefs where they belong, in the museum.

First, think of something you believe without question. For example the home you live in or the colour of your hair. As you begin to focus on this absolute statement of fact, start to be aware of what comes into your mind. What do you see, what do you hear, how does it make you feel? Remember the work we have already covered on sub-modalities in chapter one.

Notice what you notice. Notice the quality of the sub-modalities, things like, louder or softer, still or moving, brighter or dimmer. As you notice what you notice, make a note of them. Now go through the same process for something that you do not believe.

An example could be that your neighbours are aliens from the planet Zorb or that Mickey mouse is a real mouse. As before, start to look at, listen to and feel what you feel. Notice what you notice about how you're representing this non-belief. Make a note of the sub-modalities, in all the areas of sight, feeling and sound.

Now as you compare the two lists, you will notice some big differences.

You may have been associated in one representation and dissociated in the other. Your feelings may be far stronger in one than the other. Whatever the differences were for you, you now have clear distinctions to guide you between what is belief and what is a disbelief. What is real and what you allowed yourself to be frozen by.

With this new knowledge, think of a belief you were holding that you now know not to be true. One that was holding you back, but you're now free of.

Start to consider a goal or outcome you would like. Now move yourself through time, through all the steps in detail required to get to your desired goal or outcome, to a point where you can see yourself having achieved this goal, keeping a strong unwavering self-belief throughout the process.

Notice what you notice. Tap into your sub-modalities and enjoy all the great sensations associated with this achievement. What are you feeling, seeing, and hearing? Whatever it is, turn it all up.

Neuroscience research tells us that mental rehearsal in this way creates new neural pathways, as if you had actually experienced the goal already, making achieving the goal easier and....faster.

These enhanced sub-modalities will correspond to the actual experiences when the goal becomes your reality. Start to work straight away at all the actions you can take to make this happen. Believe!

YOU ARE UNIQUE

In this exercise, you can expand on your earlier work. Reflect on your life in a quiet relaxed environment and add to or make a new list of all your strengths, great qualities and the values that make YOU unique. The special person that you are.

If you initially find this difficult, do persevere! You could also go to friends you respect and trust, or people who love you and ask them to give you two or three helpful or positive qualities that they have seen demonstrated or displayed by you. Thank them and do believe them. Don't be surprised when people compliment you in areas that you hadn't realised or were unaware of, or had just taken for granted.

When you start to look through the list, notice how your perceived beliefs start to shift to the real you, as well as how much more positive and confident you feel.

PERSONAL MISSION STATEMENT

You could also go one step further. If it feels right for you and you want to, or you are motivated to discover the truth of your existence, you can start by exploring your personal mission in life.

Consider from the list of your values the ones that really reflect you. Maybe one where you spend time or would like to spend more, if you had it. Now identify and list your key strengths or talents that you have used in the past, or ones you could develop. They may even be ones others have made you more aware of to help you establish your purpose.

What would be satisfying, stimulating or meaningful for you?
What intuitive thoughts do you have?
What gives you inner motivation and energy?

It was Aristotle who said, "Where your talents and the needs of the world meet, lies your calling".

It may help you now to write a personal mission statement. A statement that reflects what you want to achieve, stand for or a compelling way of life you're being drawn to. Don't get too hung up on it if not. Now you have planted the seed, the more thought you give it, the clearer your mission will become.

Look too for inspiration from others you respect or admire. This may show a way forward for you.

From some of the quotes selected for the, "More food for thought", section at the back of the book, it will become clear to you those individuals who have found their true calling in life, their personal mission, their passion and inspiration.

Seek, and you too will find.

❖ FOOD FOR THOUGHT ❖

1. Our values are what make us unique. They are at the heart of our being.
2. Spend time to think about and list your values, what's really important to you. Better awareness and understanding can help prevent internal conflicts.
3. We are all unique. Others may have different values. Try to be more flexible and less judgemental.
4. Feelings are linked to emotions, so you will know when you're out of alignment.
5. Belief is so powerful that when harnessed positively, you can achieve greatness and A BRIGHTER FUTURE.
6. "If you believe you can, or believe you can't, you're right." Henry Ford
7. By using sub-modalities, you can distinguish between real and perceived beliefs and build a strong self-belief.

Meeting that life coach
has really helped his confidence!

CHAPTER 3

CONFIDENCE AND SELF-ESTEEM

Recently I was talking with someone on the phone for the first time and I couldn't help but notice the confident bounce in their voice as they spoke, each word had strength, yet also an empathy.

What is it, that makes confident people, confident?

I am sure the majority of you are likely to have met one or even more individuals throughout your life that have made a really positive impact on you. Their enthusiasm and zest for life can be felt in their words and seen in their facial gestures and smile. They have a charisma and you enjoy being in their company. You may even feel a great buzz and special rapport when with them. Talking with them and listening to their stories can be spellbinding. Time can stand still and it is almost as if their confidence and enthusiasm rubs off on you.

How can they be so confident? Nothing seems to phase them. Watching from a distance whatever they tackle in their life or business they appear to achieve with flying colours. It must be down to luck, mustn't it?

Whether you believe confident individuals are born with it or that confidence was nurtured, (there are various studies to show it can actually be a bit of both), you cannot get away from the fact that we are all born with a level of natural ability and a level of confidence. We had no knowledge that would make us anything else.

As babies we embarked on a journey of self-discovery, learning from our parents, guardians, family, other children and eventually teachers. We all start out with enough confidence to crawl, then walk. So why is it some people, young and adult, stand out from the crowd, while others shy away?

What gives these trailblazers the confidence to carry out tasks that many of us would cringe at and pass by? Why also, do some people have an abundance of self-esteem, of high self-worth, whilst others allow anxiety to shape their lives?

CONFIDENT THINKING

The answer is not as complicated as you would THINK and actually lies in this sentence. Once again it's about thinking and more importantly our strategy for thinking. It's about the way we experience life through our own eyes, ears and feelings. It's about how we have personally interpreted the information we have been given to date. It's about our beliefs and the emotions we have attached to them. It is also about conditioning.

For example, how a dismissive sentence here and there, especially from someone we look up to, may have affected our internal thoughts and behaviour. Being repeatedly told you're useless or rubbish at something can become a conditioned belief, creating a really unhelpful emotional state, when in reality nothing could be further from the truth.

Just spend a moment thinking about this point. Remember a time perhaps at work or maybe even at school, when someone embarrassed you in front of others, telling you how useless or pathetic you were at a task or how stupid you looked, and how on hearing this you actually believed it to be true, until you realised maybe years later, what utter rubbish they had been talking.

It's not always what a parent says to their child that makes them cry, it's often the way its being said. We often forget that communication is not just the words we use, it's about our body language, the look on our face, as well as the way it's said. Young children need constant praise and positive feedback and to be given an opportunity to try new things, to be encouraged and to experience successes, especially small first steps.

However, not all the learning models absorbed by us are positive. So as babies become children and children become adults, we have been subject to vast amounts of information to collect and process, things said to us in all sorts of ways, that we may well have misinterpreted then and continue to do so today.

Our brains are our very own computer, but will only work as well as the programs we put into it. In other words, the software programmes in our brains that we have collected along the way, could and often do hold us back, making us feel inadequate or miserable. This can then lead to a lack of self-esteem or confidence and all because we are playing software that was misread, negative, redundant or obsolete.

I have coached people who grew up thinking how useless they were because of what adults had said to them as a child. This in turn had a dramatic effect on their confidence and self-esteem for years. If any of the above has held you back, this can stop right now!! Right this very minute.

The great news is we can recode our thinking. Just like the de-cluttering of our home, we can de-clutter our thinking. We can replace brain software that has created these old or imagined beliefs that limit us or has drained our self-worth, with new exciting programs that create energy. This energy gives greater confidence, setting us towards a more rewarding and compelling future.

This is because all behaviour and thinking has structure, structure that once identified can be understood and changed. Remember the times you have talked yourself out of something because you didn't feel confident, or frightened or embarrassed that you might not succeed? Becoming more aware of your unhelpful thoughts acts as a reminder that you can press the stop button at any time. You are in control, no one else.

Rediscover how powerful positive conversations with yourself can be. You only have to watch athletes you admire, psyching themselves up before a big event to realise its power. Talking to yourself inwardly will give you a benchmark on a way forward, a way to check on your emotions. Tap into the power of positive self-talk. It will boost your confidence and can move your life forward to where you want to be.

How we all feel on the inside is played out in our lives on the outside. It's also about how much we like and value ourselves. Our thoughts play out in our lives. Feeling anxious or tied up inside affects what we project outwardly.

In order to feel good about yourself, be proud to be you and your reflection. Begin by looking inside yourself. Remember, you and you alone have control of your thoughts and your feelings. By going through the following exercises you can build and build on your confidence and self-esteem.

We are all unique. We each have special qualities and as we start to remember and reflect on them we will feel our confidence grow and feel good inside. It's always been there, it is just a case of bringing it back to the surface.

We all have something to give and have moments in our lives where we felt proud, content, had a spring in our step or saw something funny where we just couldn't stop laughing. I'm sure you were feeling some good emotions at that moment – happy, confident, relaxed maybe?

WHAT MAKES YOU SPECIAL?

Take a pen and paper and start to think about your unique and special qualities. Are you caring, kind, free-spirited, principled, thoughtful, driven or considerate? What different words would describe you?

You are clearly motivated to develop yourself, to understand yourself better, so write that down, it's a great quality to have. Start to build a list and keep adding to it. Are you adventurous, creative, loving, bold, artistic or articulate?

Think about all you have ever achieved, been proud of or something nice that someone said about you. Don't be modest, this is about you, for you and will give you a boost as you add each word or sentence. If it would help, as with the values exercise, talk to friends or people who love or care about you and ask them for two or three qualities they admire and have seen demonstrated by you. Add these to your list. With each quality you will start to feel even better about yourself and as you begin to smile on the inside, let the smile out!

Smiling and laughing are really good for you and your overall well-being. Laughter reduces tension and stress, as well as releasing beneficial chemicals in the brain that can help create better, more enjoyable emotions.

Let's go back to our confident, charismatic, enthusiastic acquaintance or friend, or even somebody we admire with these qualities that we have read about or seen on TV. Start to look more closely at the way they talk, the language they use, their body language, their posture, the way they breathe. Start to become more aware of what makes them special or unique. Becoming aware of how others present themselves can provide really useful learning for us.

Pick someone on television, perhaps someone you like and just start to study them through new eyes. Then, after a few minutes ask yourself what you notice now, but had never noticed before. You will find this new awareness a really useful tool.

UNDERSTANDING FEARS

We all go through life with some kind of fear. Fears have a way of making us feel less confident. They can block progress and stop us in our tracks. If they are stopping you from enjoying a normal day-to-day life, you do have a choice.

In order to face our fears we need to understand them first. Some fears are healthy and can be overcome, whilst others are dangerous, life threatening and should be avoided.

We will now consider the fears that though real for you, are ones that with a shift of your thinking can disappear as if by magic. Fear of the dark, fear of failure, crowded rooms, open spaces. Fear of tackling problems head on – our fears come in all shapes and sizes.

Taking one at a time, start by examining any fears you have and begin to understand it better.

Take a moment to still yourself physically and mentally, maybe with four or five slow breaths. Focus on your fear and the limiting behaviour that you engage in because of it.

After a few moments, gently turn your attention to your physical body. Where in your body is your fear located? Notice where there is tension or other uncomfortable physical sensations in your body.

How does it make you feel?

What are your thoughts about this uncomfortable sensation?

Ask yourself what the message is that you need to hear from the physical discomfort caused by your fear. Is your fear trying to protect you, keep you out of danger or is there another purpose?

There is always a positive intention behind our behaviours. Sometimes however, these good intentions can conflict with each other causing us confusion. Whenever we feel confusion, it is likely that there is an internal conflict somewhere.

The term used in Neuro-Linguistic Programming (NLP) for this internal argument is known as "conflicting parts".

Our fears, for example, could at times conflict with our confidence.

Fear of the unknown in a normally confident person for example, could bring about a state of confusion, when that generally confident person attempts or considers going into a previously unknown situation. The confusion arises as a result of the internal conflict between the two parts of safety versus confidence.

The positive intention of the safety part on one hand, trying to keep you in a zone of comfort, one you know well, one that poses no risk or threat. Whilst on the other hand, the confident part with its equally positive intention may be pushing you to a new exciting level of success or freedom.

So the confident part pushes for this new freedom and the safety part pushes equally hard against it in order to keep you safe. One wants freedom from danger. The other wants freedom from limitation.

CONFLICTING PARTS

If you are in a state of confusion, a really useful exercise is to examine and question each conflicting part, one at a time. If it helps, ask your imagination to support you, then place them one on each hand.

Start with your confident part and as it sits on your dominant hand, notice what you notice. Is it heavy or light, how does it feel, how would you describe it?

Now do the same with the conflicting part on your non-dominant hand. Compare the differences between the two.

Then ask each in turn, "what is your highest positive intention for me?"

Listen to the answer and then keep asking, "what is your highest positive intention for me?"

Do this with both parts in turn and notice what happens as you repeat and repeat the process. You will soon realise that they actually both want the same thing for you, they are just coming at it from different perspectives.

Once you have reached the same highest positive intention for each part, bring your hands together, bringing the strength of the positive intentions of both parts together as one. A new, dynamic, positive and confident intention that is no longer internally conflicted.

Now think of a time in the future when you can use this new awareness you have just harnessed. Imagine the new freedom and success it will bring as your internal team of positive intentions are all moving in the same direction.

By learning more about our fears, we can start to overcome them. Has a fear that you hold been overcome by someone else you know? If so, what did they do to overcome it? What did they say to themselves or do differently to bring about change? What internal resource or strength did they bring to the situation?

Do you perhaps have those resources too, but just never thought of using them? Find out what worked for others in overcoming their fears and see if trying those things could work for you too.

This a totally safe and holistic way of changing the internal representation we have (see the chapter on Our map of the world).

Facing our fears on our own often seems worse than facing them with good friends or loved ones. Talk about your fears to them. In addition, talking positively to ourselves can in many cases be enough to overcome some of the fears we hold. Changing our outlook and shifting a misheld belief can free us of past barriers. Some people have also found prayer a way of eliminating their fears. However, for those whose fears are deep rooted, using a counsellor or therapist for additional support could be a way forward.

MODELLING EXCELLENCE

The more confident you become, the less you fear. Modelling excellence in any field, be it sport, work or hobbies you are interested in, can set you on a more fulfilled road and is what has been done over many years with all sorts of people, with fantastic life enhancing results.

As mentioned above, start to act "as if...". For example, if you want to improve your diet, start to act as if you are already the size you would like to be. Look at the clothes you would be wearing, model the person who has already achieved what you are setting out to do. Watch the way they walk and see yourself walking with the same spring in your step and enjoying the same healthy diet. The more you channel your positive energy in this way, two things happen. One, you become more naturally confident and happier and two, you will achieve great results faster.

If you want to be a public speaker, start to model the behaviours of those you admire and respect. Start to act as if you are a public speaker. See yourself in front of a roomful of friendly faces, hear yourself speaking confidently and look at the responsive look on the faces of your audience. It will not take away your own identity, just give you a better result and extra confidence to shine.

NEW BEHAVIOUR GENERATOR

The exercise below is called the, "New Behaviour Generator", and gives a step by step guide to bringing a positive change you're seeking, be it new behaviour or an improvement of a current situation.

Firstly, decide what new behaviour you want to learn or what you want to improve. What is your goal?

Now ask yourself, how would I look and sound if I were doing things exactly as I wanted, what would be different? If for example you were trying to improve in a sport, what would be different from the current situation that you're in?

Feel yourself begin to relax.

Think about your breathing and as you do so construct a visual image, allowing the pictures to form in your mind, looking up and seeing yourself performing exactly as you want, confidently, displaying that skill or new behaviour.

If you find this difficult to do at this stage, think of someone you admire or respect that does this well and watch them in your imagination, then try the skills out for yourself. By acting, "as if", you now have the resources that they are demonstrating or displaying.

Play out the movie in your mind, it's your movie. Is there anything you could do to make it even better? Be your own film director and edit away, until you're completely happy with it.

Once you're satisfied with your movie, play it again, but this time I want you to imagine its actually you, doing what you saw, associated in the picture, in your movie and associated with the feelings. How does it make you feel? If it feels right, enjoy the feelings, if not, go back a few steps and look and see yourself performing again exactly as you want. Make any adjustments, then progress through the exercise again.

When you're happy with your movie and your leading role performance, think of what trigger you can use to remind you of using this new resource at a future time or event. Think of a future event, then set off the trigger. This will do two things. One, allow you to enjoy the new positive feelings and two, confirm the new resource is in place, giving you a new way and new choices in the future.

Imagine new freedom to make even more choices and live the life that you want to live. More confidence will enable you to do things you have always wanted to do, but weren't ready to attempt – your preparation is under way.

"When you have confidence, you can have a lot of fun. And when you have fun you can do amazing things." (Author unknown).

"If you hear a voice within you say, 'you cannot paint', then by all means paint, and that voice will be silenced." Vincent Van Gough

TURBOCHARGE YOUR CONFIDENCE

Sit somewhere quiet and away from distractions. Begin to get comfortable and start to relax. Take a deep breath and exhale, in through the nose and out through the mouth. That's right, you can feel yourself starting to become more comfortable with each deep breath you take.

Take your breath in, filling your stomach first, then your chest, with long deep breaths. Breathing on the in breath to the slow count of three and on the out breath to the slow count of six.

As you concentrate on your breathing and you relax even more, why not start to think of how things would be for you if you were more confident and how helpful that could be to you.

Begin by recalling a past experience. An experience of feeling confident or if this is difficult, you could borrow the characteristics from someone you know. Someone you admire or respect, someone who has all the resources that you want. Borrow these confident characteristics and try them on for size.

Before moving on, start to play out the movie in your mind, the movie where you have recaptured the confident memory or you are borrowing the confident resource. Now, act "as if" it's you in the movie. You being confident, you having this resource and associate into it fully. Notice what you notice, "as if" you were there again. See again now what you saw, hear again now what you heard and feel again now what you felt. Feel your body being tension free, in a confident position.

Breathing deep and relaxed, with a brilliant beautiful smile coming from deep inside. As you are experiencing this wonderfully confident you, fully and vibrantly, simply clench your fist and say to yourself the word "WOW!"

Now think of a situation or event that you want to be confident in and one which will be happening in your life soon or sometime in the near future. Imagine that event now and put yourself into the picture. See the fully confident you enjoying the moment. What are you saying to others, to yourself?

Notice how you are breathing. What's your posture like? Are you sitting or standing, what expression do you have on your face? How are others interacting with you? There's no rush, just enjoy the movie.

Make the picture bolder, brighter, clearer and BIGGER.

Again, associate into the fully confident you, this time by firing your anchor, simply by clenching your fist and saying "WOW!"

Now...

Hear what you hear.

See what you see.

Feel what you feel.

Let all those good, vibrant, fully alive, confident feelings into every part of your body. Let them spin, faster and faster and enjoy the moment.

As you feel the feeling starting to peak, anchor those confident feelings again as before, by clenching the same fist and saying to yourself "WOW!"

Now, whenever you want to bring a boost to your confidence, it's right there for you. All you have to do is to fire your anchor by clenching your fist and saying "WOW" to yourself. All those good, vibrant, confident feelings will return into every part of you.

As you come back to the here and now, you become aware of the room and notice how energised you feel. You can think about how all your great qualities make you feel proud to be you.

You now have a positive memory of being confident in the future event. Enjoy it!

Smile on the inside. Now let your beaming, bright smile out.

Go through the exercise again soon, tomorrow if possible.

The more times you go through this process, the easier it will be to call up the behaviour you want and the more you, and others will notice your new levels of confidence.

This is a form of mental rehearsal. Modern neuroscience has shown that repeated rehearsal of detailed states and behaviours form new neural pathways and structures in the brain and so the brain is already familiar with the "behaviour".

It has already been learned, so it is easily recalled and utilized when needed.

❖ FOOD FOR THOUGHT ❖

1. We are all born with a level of confidence and natural ability.
2. Grow to like yourself, the you that is really you. If we feel good inside, we project that feeling outwards. Other people react more favourably and that boosts our confidence.
3. Build a list of your unique and special qualities. Keep adding to the list.
4. To face your fears, start to understand them.
5. Modelling excellence in others enables you to replicate their behaviour "as if" it were your own and boosts your own confidence.
6. The New Behaviour Generator is a step by step guide to bring about the positive changes you're seeking.
7. The confidence turbocharger is new software to replace old programs.
8. You and you alone, are in control of your thoughts and the actions you take in your future.

CHAPTER 4

OVERCOMING OBSTACLES

Obstacles are part of everyday life and have been since the beginning of time. They come in all shapes and sizes – health, well-being, work, lifestyle, relationships with others. They all have something in common – a need to be addressed one way or another.

Whether it's snow preventing you from driving to work or catching a flight (as I write this chapter the UK has been hit by the worst December weather for over 100 years), or financial hardship; obstacles will never be far away. (If your obstacles are often people based, you will find the paragraph on rapport really useful).

VISIBLE VS PERCEIVED OBSTACLES

Just ask any salesperson about the number of different obstacles (they call them objections) he or she faces on a daily basis. There are however only two types. Those that are real, visible and can impact on us and those we perceive to be there but only actually exist in our own minds. The great news is that by changing our thinking we can have a positive experience from both the real and perceived obstacles.

Let's take visible obstacles first. It was Michael Jordan, the basketball player who said, "Obstacles don't have to stop you. If you run into a wall, don't give up and turn around. Figure out how to climb it, go through it or work around it."

To me, this statement demonstrates several things. Firstly that we have various options, so it's really useful to weigh them all up before embarking on a particular course of action, one which might take up the most amount of time, use the most resources and be the least effective.

There's more than one way...

...to overcome life's obstacles!

Options are often plentiful, but many of us rush ahead without thinking for a moment and taking even just a little time to consider how many options we can come up with to overcome the obstacle we are faced with.

If this sounds like you and you're able to make successful snap decisions every time, you are one of the lucky few, as most of us would benefit from considering a number of options before deciding on the most appropriate course of action. In the Goal Setting chapter, the Grow Model demonstrates how important and effective considering options is, and is key to the framework within coaching individuals.

I often have clients who when considering the question of, "what options do you have", come up with two or three ideas, but when I give them a few more moments to think then ask, "and anything else", will suddenly come up with a brilliant option, one that was in their unconscious thoughts rather than conscious.

The next point demonstrated by Jordan was his flexibility. At times we all want to stand firm, we have our opinion and we're not interested in another view. In other words we think we know best and aren't prepared to budge. Open-minded flexibility though, helped Jordan's thinking and enabled him to see a way around the obstacle.

We will cover more about flexibility later in the book, as its impacts are far reaching, but as an example, in NLP there are a list of 13 pre-suppositions, one of which relates to flexibility. Let us pre-suppose you are totally flexible, it doesn't necessarily have to be true, but if it were as the pre-supposition states, "the person with the most flexibility wins the day." Being entrenched and making a stand, making a point, allowing no flexibility, will often produce just that.

No flexibility = no resolution = no movement forward.

This can and often does place people in a non-productive emotional state - upset, wound-up, frustrated, or worse still, angry or ill.

Thirdly, Jordan had a positive approach to the obstacle. Tackling obstacles with purpose and a positive attitude is often all it takes to win the day. From the options he selected a way forward, a way to move in his case around the obstruction. He was motivated to achieve.

Thinking positive thoughts produces positive results from our actions.

Some people see all obstacles as a problem, or worse still a nightmare. They may spend so much energy and time worrying, often unnecessarily, but the consequences, as I have already mentioned can make them angry, exhausted and ill.

Others embrace obstacles as a challenge, something that makes them feel good inside when they have overcome them.

Once again, it's all in our thinking.

You can choose how you want to feel by re-framing your thoughts. Obstacles seem less frightening when we view them positively, when we see them for what they really are, a chance to help us grow, an opportunity to shine.

Overcoming obstacles can build our confidence and deepen our character. It's all a question of the spin you put on it. Start to see obstacles for what they really are – an opportunity to learn, an opportunity for receiving a feeling of achievement when they are overcome, not just as a pain in the backside! Obstacles might even become something you welcome.

Think back to a time when you were faced with an obstacle or challenge that scared you, but the actions you took worked for you. Yet it was one that might have seemed impossible at the time. You don't remember all the details, only that you survived it and lived to tell the tale. It made you stronger.

PEOPLE OBSTACLES

I am sure like me there have been many occasions where you have witnessed how people can stand in the way of others, sometimes unknowingly, sometimes not, but they all leave you with the same feeling, frustration or at worst anger. From the unhelpful receptionist at the doctor's surgery, to the person at a company or call centre refusing to put you through to a decision maker. Some people even experience these type of blocks and obstacles within their own family, preventing them from talking to those they would like.

In many of these cases obstacles can be broken down if we take the initiative, are more flexible with our approach and utilise the rapport techniques contained within this book.

Another block or obstacle is the one that we create in our own minds. We start to believe without any foundation, things that just aren't true. These beliefs are limiting and can stop us moving forward or trying something new. How often have you been faced with a challenge where you start to tell yourself, "I can't do this or that", "I don't have enough skills to tackle this problem", only to find that not only you could do it, but do it really well!

What went on? Have you ever stopped to think about it? The first thing that happened was that a limiting belief crept in and in your own mind you started to believe all sorts of things that were not true, then blew them out of proportion.

On that occasion you then overcame the self-doubts and to good effect. You re-framed the challenge and started to become more confident in your ability to resolve the obstacle. You allowed your unconscious to help show you the way. By thinking through your options and maybe having an inspired thought, you overcame the issue. Try to understand the successful internal thinking strategy you used then, as you can call on it again, any time in the future.

There's another game that goes on in our minds, it's called mind chatter. Like a tennis match where we start to think about doing something new – it could be a hobby or business idea, possibly even asking someone on a date, or many other things, only to allow our conscious mind to come up with all the reasons as to why we shouldn't do it. We put ourselves down, allow the negative self-talk to win the day, never begin to explore the possibilities or enjoy many of the things that would enhance our lives and give us fun – a new relationship perhaps or a new experience.

What a waste! All because our internal dialogue (mind chatter) wouldn't shut up long enough for us to give it a try. These negative thoughts can at times make us freeze on the spot or create a fear so strong that we don't pursue our goals or dreams. Literally talking ourselves out of doing something before we've got even near to doing it.

What you are doing (in this instance mind chatter), definitely isn't working for you – so do something different!

After all...

If you always do what you've done, you'll always get what you've got!

I said there was more great news earlier and here it is. You were also given a clue when I asked you to start thinking about your own successful internal strategies.

The news is YOU have control of your thoughts and can banish these limiting beliefs simply by using your brain software in a more effective way.

You can re-programme how and what you think really really quickly.

If you hear negative self-talk, simply speed it up so that it sounds like Mickey Mouse, or has a really funny tone attached to it. A sort of "na na didly na na" tone. You know the one, one that makes you smile inside. Does it sound so serious now?

Even now you can go further by sending the sound off...way into the distance, until it can no longer be heard. Notice how your physiology and emotions change in response to the previous limiting self-talk, simply by changing the tone, speed and volume of it.

Along with everything else you have become more aware of as you read this chapter, the following exercise will put you firmly back in the driving seat so that you can tackle obstacles with confidence, change a strong negative belief into an empowering one and take your life wherever you want to go.

If you have had an experience in your life that still affects you negatively, a trauma would be one for example, or maybe as a result of a poor decision you made, this Decision Destroyer Process exercise created by Richard Bandler can neutralise it here and now.

DECISION DESTROYER PROCESS

First, begin by thinking of a positive and empowering memory, one so empowering that it impacts positively on your behaviour today.

It's a memory that formed a positive imprint, maybe when you were younger, maybe later in life, but you don't question it, you just know it's true. It may reflect a core value or be part of you in another way, but as you focus on this positive and powerful memory, start to relive it, as if happening now, right this minute.

Associate into this memory. See what you saw then, through your own eyes, as if seeing it again now. Hear what you heard and feel what you felt.

Check out the features for later comparison. Notice all the detail. How bright the picture is, all the colours. Maybe it's black or white; moving or still, near............or far away. Are the sounds LOUD or quiet? What internal feelings are you attaching to it?

You may find it useful to write down all the different facets of each sense to assist you.

(Each of these divisions of detail is called sub-modality. Modalities being the name given to the particular sense you are experiencing and then using internally to retrieve information). I cover this in more detail in Chapter One.

Now I want you to think of an ordinary memory, one that doesn't affect your life one way or another. Think back to yesterday perhaps, walking into work, or opening a window. Once again, note down the details of the sub-modalities.

Now start to compare these memories and the sub-modalities of them. What sub-modalities are creating the power in your positive empowering memory? Is it bright or dull? Does it have colour? Is it bigger or more dramatic than the ordinary memory?

Take a few moments to notice the differences, even jot them down if that helps. If you were going to make it into a movie, what are all the tiny qualities that would make it a blockbuster?

Think about the sound quality, the picture quality and anything else that makes it the great empowering memory pattern that it is.

When you have total clarity, I want you to picture yourself holding the movie as a reel of the blockbuster you've just made, with all the great colours, sounds and feelings attached to it. Now go on a journey in your mind, or better still, by physically standing and taking a walk along your time line. (Time lines are explored in detail in the chapter on Time).

Travel back in time, back along your time line, until you arrive at a point in your past where this positive empowering memory can be placed just before the negative or traumatic memory you encountered.

Keep focused on your positive imprint, remain associated with it and start to rapidly move forward in time, taking this positivity with you as you move through and beyond the negative time. See, hear and feel how that event is transformed. Notice how the old problem imprint experience is transformed and re-evaluated.

Keep moving forward quickly, to the present, the hear and now. Notice how all the past memories are changing and being enriched with your positive, exciting blockbuster imprint.

Now, stop for a moment, dissociate from the experience, then picture yourself with this positive imprint, moving forward in your life, through your future experiences, seeing what you will be doing differently as a result of this experience.

As you plan your future, think about when this new, enriching, positive thought pattern will be of most use to you and make a mental note. A powerhouse of positivity being used to combat any obstacles that dare try to get in your way.

ANCHORING

Although the term anchoring may not be familiar to you, it impacts every one of us every day. Just think of the smell of egg and bacon cooking, or a Sunday roast, or many other things that link our senses with a past event.

We all have these triggers that can move our emotions. A favourite piece of music for some, watching or even scoring a winning goal, a precious memory, a photo, a special place, and many other things. They transport us back to a really happy moment of time in our life.

Just the other day I was sitting at the traffic lights waiting my turn, when in front of me an old 60's Ford Popular drove past. In that moment I was 6 again. My Dad had bought this model as our first family car and we went out on trips and took holidays in it. I relived the excitement I felt all those years ago as if it was yesterday.

Positive anchors are really useful from moving you from an unwanted or unhelpful emotional state to a better place, as quickly as you can think about them. You can even anchor positive feelings to a place on your body, as quickly as touching your ear lobe or elbow. This turbo-boost of positive energy is there whenever you need to call on it.

You may like to read through the following exercise before carrying it out.

SETTING A POSITIVE ANCHOR

Begin by thinking about a positive internal resource that would be useful to you in the future. What word describes it?

Hold that thought. Now sit down and begin to think how re-energizing it is to relax. Breathe slowly and deeply or use this breathing technique. Breath in for 4 seconds, hold your breath for 4 seconds, now breathe out for 4 seconds. Do this again.

As you start to relax more and more and get even more comfortable, you notice how comfy the chair has become. You may even wish to close your eyes. You now start to think of a time when you overcame a particular obstacle in your life and how good it felt then to achieve this. A time where you were in control, confident in yourself, your decisions, and a time where you displayed this resource in your life.

Start to remember that time vividly. What did you see? What was happening? What feelings did you have? What did you hear? Think about how you were breathing.... and breathe now, just as you were then. Use all of your senses to capture all the great, happy, confident emotions.

As you relive those feelings, all those good feelings and really enjoy the moment, make the picture bigger and brighter. Allow all those good feelings to wash over you from your toes to your head, swirling all around your body. As the moment peaks, and you will know when, you can anchor all those good feelings, allowing you to have this powerful resource at your fingertips whenever you need it.

Perhaps place your finger and thumb on your ear lobe and squeeze gently or lightly touch your elbow. You decide, and as you do so remember you had all the resources and motivation to overcome the obstacle then and you have even more resources now.

This new awareness will make all your obstacles so much easier to deal with now you understand that they are there to help you grow and live a better life. As you start to bring yourself back into the room, notice how relaxed you feel and ready to enjoy the rest of your day.

Now think about a time in the future when this anchor of resource would be useful, and as you think clearly about this future event, fire your anchor and notice the different modalities of it. This is called future pacing.

If it worked properly you will relive all the good, positive resourceful feelings. If not, don't worry, just go back to the start of the exercise and re-fire the anchor when all the good feelings peak.

You can add more resource anchors by using this technique, but always be sure to future pace and test them, to ensure they work properly for you.

It was Jack Penn who said, "One of the greatest secrets of life is to make stepping stones out of stumbling blocks."

❖ FOOD FOR THOUGHT ❖

1. Accept that obstacles are part of life, an opportunity for us to learn and grow.
2. Use the GROW model to think about all the possible options, before deciding the best course of action to take.
3. Be flexible in your approach to obstacles, and people.
4. Thinking positive thoughts produces positive results from our actions.
5. The decision destroyer neutralises negative trauma and replaces it with an empowering pattern.
6. Use anchoring to gain additional positive resources and boost your confidence and motivation.
7. Trust your unconscious. It will help if you let it.

There's more than one way...

...to enjoy success!

CHAPTER 5

GOAL SETTING

I have met many people over the years with a real hang up about setting goals. Let's just wait and see what happens, go with the flow, say some, whilst others have said, "I have never been any good at this sort of thing, so why bother."

These comments are often typical and when you consider that many employers use and impose unrealistic targets on individuals and teams without giving the necessary support, then metaphorically beat them up for missing them, it's easy to see why.

Goal setting reluctance could also be due to an unsuccessful attempt at something in the past. Not being selected for the school team or not taking up a new hobby because we didn't think we were good enough. An old unhelpful memory playing out in our mind from a past experience where we tried and it didn't work out well. Maybe embarrassment set in, so we talk ourselves out of going after the life we would really like. The don't rock the boat, I'll only get disappointed syndrome. However, our attitude is key to the achievement of our goals.

WHY SET GOALS?

Although we may not label them as such, we already set goals and make life choices.

Remember the time you wanted a particular room in the house decorated by Christmas, or that new piece of furniture or carpet in place before a special event. You may even prepare a shopping list of things you need before heading into town. Or maybe you want to get fitter for a forthcoming holiday? Well, you had a goal, the motivation and a, "by when", time attached to it. You also had a positive approach towards it. In other words, you had a positive attitude.

In this chapter I will show you how to build on this process. I will teach you more about setting goals, how to achieve them and help you to understand the real power of goal setting, as well as how this formula can be applied to your life to help you live the life you really want, and stay the course.

TAKING POSITIVE ACTION

First, goal setting should be fun, exciting and press what I call your hot button. Something that produces positive motivation and drive.

Trust the process. It works, and I promise you, it does produce results. There is nothing that gives me greater satisfaction than seeing clients achieving their goals. When you too start to see the results you can achieve, it will become a fundamental part of your life from now on.

I have been setting myself both personal and business goals for over 40 years and I am still learning! I continue to enjoy the process and the results. It's a way of life, a habit and I still smile every time I review my goals and can tick off another achievement.

Goals are for you and about you. Something you want to achieve or experience. They are not something you want others to do or they want you to do. Goals need ownership and only you can only take responsibility for your own personal goals.

There is a well defined process to goal setting and without follow through so many people trip themselves up, then give up.

Let's take the New year's resolution as an example. This year some will say, "I am going to get fit." So individuals join health clubs by the thousand, with the best intentions. Some run out of steam after just a few days, but normally by Easter the enthusiastic new members have mostly gone. It has been this way for the past 20 years at the health club my wife and I go to. Every January the new flurry and by Easter all back to normal. A few new faces remain, but most have long since gone.

Why is this? Well for some, genuine work or family pressures might have got in the way, but for the majority, there was no plan, no real strategy for the goal, little action, low motivation. Just a resolution and a wish.

Goals come in all shapes and sizes. Some are short term, some are longer and can be set for any reason, at any time of the year. Over many years, I have set goals for both business and personal reasons, for health and well-being, for financial and material and for giving structure, purpose and direction to my life.

One key to achieving goals that I will expand on again later is that big or long term goals need to be broken down into manageable chunks if they are to be achieved.

For instance, I remember sometime ago talking with a neighbour who had a couple of rooms that needed some re-decorating. His walls needed some tidying and painting, yet the very thought of the whole task initially gave him zero motivation. I encouraged him to consider all the options and following a brief discussion he decided to a) break the goal down into sections and b) take action within the next week, as it was likely to be far easier to get the job done than think up even more novel and creative excuses to try out on his wife.

The following weekend he set some goals and took action. He made a list, bought the paint and materials and progressed with one wall at a time. Later he told me that his motivation not only increased, but he actually began to enjoy the task. The job got done far quicker than he had thought possible and looked great. The goal he undertook and achieved might appear insignificant, however the principles used work in exactly the same way, be they small or huge.

A goal that's daunting for you even if realistic, can become more compelling, more motivational and give you the drive to take action if you break it down into segments, as well as give you the track to run on.

Motivation and action are key to the achievement of every goal. Keep looking at ways that you can be enthusiastic about a goal. Ask yourself, "what will it do for me when achieved?" If it doesn't hit your hot button, come at it from another angle until it does. Keep gaining momentum and maintain a positive attitude.

Picture in your mind the world's strongest man competition, where they have to pull a lorry by rope over a certain distance. From a stand still position, they need to get the momentum to get started. Once rolling it gets easier, but great focus, energy and a can do attitude were needed to get moving, and to stay motivated to achieve their goal.

GROW MODEL

A cornerstone in all the coaching work taught at The Coaching Academy and a technique I continue to use today, is called the G R O W model.

The G stands for Goal.
This is where the goal becomes clearly defined and this is what moves it from the wish list to a goal with a purpose, a goal with clarity. Ask yourself, "what will it mean to me if I achieve this goal?" How does it make me feel? How challenging or exciting is it?

R is for Reality.
It has to be real for you. A good question to ask yourself is what resources do you have or need that would help you in the achievement of the goal? Another might be, what is happening in your life now that is good which might help contribute towards the outcome? What is important to you?

O is for Options.

Here you have an opportunity to let your thinking run free. Get a pen and paper and just brainstorm. Write down everything that comes to mind. Don't stop until you have several options, even if some are far out, write them down!

Don't allow yourself to start analysing them at this stage as it will stop your creative thoughts. List everything you could do, but not necessarily will. Something I often get my clients to do is to take a clean sheet of paper, draw a circle in the middle, now write the goal in the circle.

Thinking about the goal, start to think about all the different options there may be to achieve it. Draw little lines in any direction you like, then add words or draw pictures. This will produce a mind map and there's an example of one in the Law Of Attraction chapter. Let your imagination run free – this will often produce some really helpful options for your list.

When you have finished, try to think of one or two more options. Now think about how a friend might tackle the goal and add these ideas to the list. You now have a sheet of many options to select from. Pick the two or three ideas that you can work with, ideas that will move you towards your goal.

W is for the Way forward.

This is the course of action you plan to take. The what, by when etc... Test your level of motivation by asking yourself this question.

On a scale of 1 to 10 – one being little motivation and ten being....bring it on, where do you sit?

If the answer is around 5 or 6, you need to re-think the goal and its importance to you.

An 8 or 9 is a good starting point, with 10 being an ideal score.

If for example you saw it as a 7, the question is what do you need to do to get to an 8 or 9? The stronger your motivation at this point, the more likely you are to see the goal through.

SMART GOALS

Another acronym associated with goal setting is that goals should be SMART:

Specific
Measurable
Achievable
Realistic
Time framed/bound

Goals need to be Specific. For example, let's say you would like to lose some weight. You specify this as your goal. Now you can move through the process to make your goal SMART.

Losing weight is specific, but not Measurable. So setting yourself a target of losing say 10 pounds is now measurable.

It also has to be Achievable for you, and Realistic. If it isn't then reset the goal until it is.

Finally, put a time frame around the goal. This could be, "I will lose 10lbs over the next 5 weeks" (or 10 weeks). Whatever is achievable and realistic for you.

These SMART steps will give you a really strong foundation to build on as you start to consider each goal.

However, before we look forward to the future, let's take stock of your journey so far. I am sure you would also be surprised at what you have already accomplished in the past twelve months, when you stop to think about it. Before moving on, why not take a few minutes out to list the things you are pleased with, the successes of your year. Think about areas in your life that have gone well, the things you are grateful for, even little milestones achieved. These past experiences can give you valuable motivation as you consider the areas in your life you want to concentrate on moving forward.

TEN STEP GOAL SETTING

If you're ready to start setting a goal or more for yourself, get a pen and pad and after relaxing for a few moments follow through my 10 point goal setting plan.

As you begin, you will see how the chapters on Law Of Attraction and Visualisation start to bring together all your positive energy and focus. With the positive efforts and actions you take in pursuing your goals, you can embark on a new journey you will enjoy and find fulfilling and rewarding.

1. Write down all the goals you would like to achieve. They might include health, work, relationships, finances, work life balance, a new experience, or something in your life you want to change. What have you always wanted to do but been too afraid to attempt? Let the list grow; keep coming back to it when you want.

   Before you read on, really do write down your goals, as those who write personal goals are 10 times more likely of achieving success than those who don't. (Harvard University study)

2. Now select a goal that is key to your overall plan, a major focus. One that can give you a win over the next 3 to 6 months. This goal must be realistic and specific. Remember SMART. Also it should fit with your personal values.

   Write this goal on a separate sheet or a postcard that you can look at daily.

It must be written in a positive and personal sentence and in present tense. For example, something like, "I am pleased now that...", or, "I enjoy my life now that...". Also, we think in pictures. If I were to say winner, you would paint a picture in your mind of a winner. So to support you further, find pictures that will help you. Even draw pictures around the goal that relate to it, then put them in a place that you will look at every day.

3. List ALL the actions you can take to move yourself closer to this goal. It is really useful to brainstorm all the ideas you come up with rather than discount them. Review the actions from the list and choose the best options that will work for you.

4. Next to your chosen actions place a time by which you want to have achieved that particular task. For example, tomorrow by 6pm or in two weeks, by 10th Feb etc.

5. Now think about what resources you need to achieve your action plan. What support do you need? What changes need to take place for you to succeed? Can you share the goal with a close friend? Do you require some training or to learn a new skill? How will you stay motivated and disciplined? What will you say to yourself to stop old limiting beliefs cluttering your thoughts?

Write everything down that comes to mind. In addition, to fully complement the models and techniques in this book you could explore other areas of learning. Audio CD's, success stories and web information that can help you stay motivated and keep you on track. If you stop learning, you stop growing.

6. Now you are committed to your Goal, start to get excited and visualise success. Picture in your mind's eye how things will be for you when you have achieved it. How will you feel? What will you hear? What will you be saying? What will have changed? The more you feel the emotion of success, the more powerful your unconscious thoughts will help to bring it about. Make the picture big and bright and enjoy the moment. Enjoy the good feelings. This will give you added motivation to stay the course.

7. Take action straight away. Break the goal into segments that will move you forward and encourage you. Do something every day that will move you closer to where you want to be. Remember, 0 effort = 0 result.

8. Review your goals regularly. Chart your progress and enjoy each success. Be aware of what you are learning about yourself and how you are handling the challenges more easily than before. Congratulate yourself on your progress.

9. Celebrate each goal as it happens. Enjoy the journey and continue to set new goals as you create the life you want.
10. Share your success with others. Be an inspiration! Your positive energy will attract!

A few additional thoughts to consider. Be flexible, open-minded and action your goal now. Wishing for a different result from little or no activity is just wishful thinking.

BRIAN TRACY GOAL EXERCISE

Another great exercise I learnt and use personally came from another of my heroes – author, coach and public speaker Brian Tracy. This will once again show you just how effective goal setting is.

Begin to think of 10 short term goals you would like to achieve over the next 12 months. Write them down in present and positive tense as before. Start each sentence with I and then put an action word, writing each sentence as if it had already happened. For example, "I have my dream job...".

Now fold up the sheet of paper and put it somewhere safe. A drawer at home or somewhere else you will remember where you put it. You can review it whenever you like but look at it again at least every month. You will be surprised at how much of the list you have achieved and realise how quickly some of the goals happened after setting them out. As you achieve your goals, keep adding new ones to your list.

THE CIRCLE OF LIFE

On the following pages I have reproduced four life circles and two examples. These are areas in your life that you may like to set personal goals in.

These circles each represent your roles or tasks in life and your life choices. By completing each circle in this graphic way you may start to notice and become more aware of areas that are out of alignment or even ruling you. You can then bring about more balance, control and harmony by targeting your goal setting. Thinking on paper can have really positive outcomes.

My Roles

With the first circle, you could think about the different roles you play in your life. Concentrate on the most important to you, the ones that take up most of your time currently. Make a list. For example you might be breadwinner, husband or wife, family member, mum or dad, son or daughter. Home-maker, friend, socialiser, decorator, gardener, fund-raiser, peacemaker. Lover, partner, boss, cleaner, carer – you will reveal several key roles that you undertake.

Now allocate a percentage of the circle to each of your roles, as per the following example. If you're spending 20% of your time in one role, and 5% in another, you still have 75% of your circle to allocate (see example 1). You could use a different colour for each role. In an instant, you will notice how much of your time is spent on each role. Is there one role that dominates the others and stops you from enjoying or being effective in others? Where would you like to spend more time? What have you noticed? Is there a role you would like to make a better impact in? Use the GROW process to help you identify what changes you could make to give you the balance you seek. Set new goals for each role. Even the smallest changes can bring about great results in other areas.

My Tasks

The next circle is useful for those who have to carry out a number of tasks, possibly even within the same role. An example of this might be in your job. You might be a receptionist, typist, caterer, marketeer, salesperson and much more. You could be in a position of responsibility. Perhaps you are a team leader. If you're running a business or are self-employed, there is any number of tasks required to be carried out on a daily basis. Again, you can use this circle to consider where your time is being spent most effectively. Is it the profitable, productive areas or those that contribute little to the bottom line? Notice what you notice. As you work through the circle, the more aware you are of the time dedicated to different tasks, the easier it will be to make positive changes.

Circle of Life

The next, but critical circle is often referred to as a wheel and it considers all the various aspects of your life. This time your circle has eight equal segments, like the spokes to a wheel. You can then give a title to each of the eight sections. They may contain Money, Health, Career, Hobbies, Sport, Recreation, Personal growth, Study, Friends, Environment, Relationships, or anything else you may choose.

Now consider the wheel as having a centre point and an outer edge. The centre point ranks as zero and the outer edge as 10. Zero represents total dissatisfaction and 10 total satisfaction (See example 2). Place an x on each spoke of the wheel, representing your satisfaction with each selected aspect of your life. Now join the x's and you have a wheel. How does it look?

This will give you a visual graph to work on. There may be areas you are really satisfied and happy with and others that you would like to focus or set goals on. Don't expect to have a perfect wheel, just focus on improving yourself. Consider that when the wheel becomes more aligned in one area it could impact on another. You now have a clear blueprint from which to work and the less distorted your wheel, the less bumpy the ride is. The more air you have in it, the smoother the journey you're taking through life.

A fourth circle has been printed for you to design and set your own goal idea.

THE CIRCLE OF LIFE

Example 1
Roles/Tasks

_____

_____

_____

_____

_____

_____

_____

_____

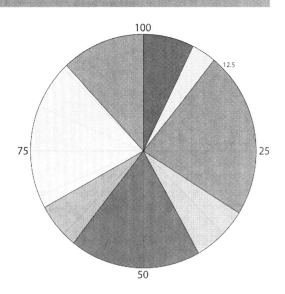

Example 2
Life Areas

_____

_____

_____

_____

_____

_____

_____

_____

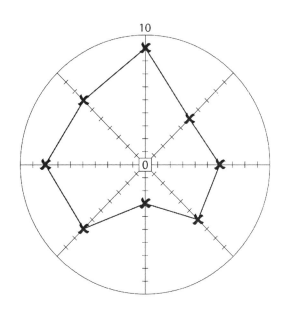

THE CIRCLE OF LIFE

Roles

_____

_____

_____

_____

_____

_____

_____

_____

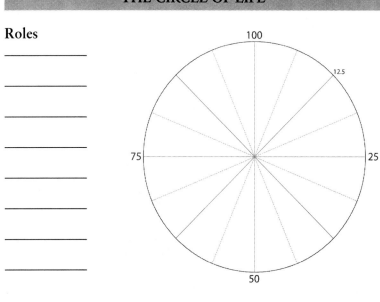

Tasks

_____

_____

_____

_____

_____

_____

_____

_____

_____

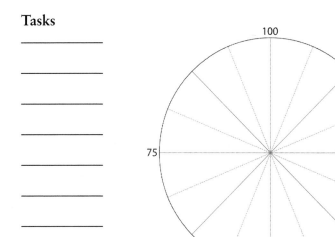

THE CIRCLE OF LIFE

Life Areas

_____

_____

_____

_____

_____

_____

_____

_____

10

0

My Goal

_____

_____

_____

_____

_____

_____

_____

_____

10

0

❖ FOOD FOR THOUGHT ❖

1. Your goals are for you and should hit your motivation hot button.
2. A written or picture goal is 10 times more likely to be achieved than others.
3. Be realistic about the goals you set and the timings. Then take action.
4. Forward pace and visualise your goals with feeling.
5. Review your goals regularly. Make changes when needed and persevere.
6. If we had no goals in life, we'd have nowhere to aim. Fulfil your potential, celebrate each step and you will surprise yourself at how quickly your hopes and dreams can become your reality.
7. Each goal starts with a thought. What are you thinking about?
8. Take action. Nothing will change until you do.

CHAPTER 6

TIME

No matter what else we can change in our lives, we all have to live within the constraints of time. On time, in time, out of time, the effects of time govern our lives, with the same number of seconds in a minute, minutes in an hour and the same number of hours in the day. It matters not whether you're starting out in life, a world leader or billionaire, we all work within these confines.

There is a monumental difference though, to how effective different individuals can be with the same amount of time. Also, where a moment of time, a second or split second may be unimportant to you or I, for a sports person it can be the difference between a gold medal or coming last. We can go ahead and waste a day without too much thought, but for the person given a week to live by their medical specialist every moment is precious.

Many people embark on time management courses, seeking answers to getting more time, only to end up disappointed with many of the tools that were supposed to make their life easier, having to make even more time to fill out the revolutionary diary that was meant to change their life but doesn't. However, the more effective we can learn to become with this precious commodity, the more time we have to focus on the things that are really important to us.

So why does a book about your thoughts and strategies to help re-focus your thinking, include a chapter all about time? Firstly, I now have you already thinking about time. Its importance, relevance and how if we could model those who are brilliant at utilising this resource to its full, we too could achieve much in our lives that we set out to and within time frames that we set.

You don't have to look far to find individuals who despite the constraints of time still achieve great things in their lives. Who do you admire, that lived or is living out their life's mission?

Secondly, by becoming more aware of how we experience time in our minds, we can plan for future goals using time lines.

Thirdly, we need to understand how we comprehend time.

For some it will be structured, organised and planned, whilst for others it's about being in the moment, the here and now, this very second. Do you like to plan a day off ahead, to know what you're doing down to the last detail, or is your map of the world to see how you feel on the day and take things as they come?

By understanding how we experience or view time, we can start to harness it more effectively, whatever map we're using to guide us.

Time externally is measured in distance and motion, but internally we all have a unique way of thinking back to access our memories that is time related. Most of us will experience the connection of past times, the present and the future as a line, often referred to as our time line.

TIME LINES

These two words may conjure up a leap into the unknown, journeys into space, Dr Who, the new frontier, back to the future, forward into space and much more. Time lines have been in existence and used by others for many centuries. Our personal time line is actually, "the memory coding", of our brain, it's one way in which we store our memories. These stored memories affect how we experience not only life itself, but also time.

Time lines have a fantastic way of supporting and guiding you on life's journey. They are a way of exploring your future, as well as recoding painful, or traumatic memories or phobias from the past. (For more on this, take a look at the Decision Destroyer in the Overcoming Obstacles chapter).

In this chapter we will use time lines to, "future pace", a way of encoding a positive success memory track for a chosen outcome. In essence, with the heightened awareness and learnings from your past and your present, you can harness this resource positively to your benefit, in future situations and goals.

Just think about how useful this would be – having a clear path to fulfilling one or more of your life's ambitions.

HOW TO CODE TIME

To begin, we need to establish your personal time line, which falls in the general categories of "in time" and "through time".

One way is to simply answer this question, "where's the past and where's the future for you?"............Or in what direction is your past?

Now point to it. What direction is your future? Again point to it.

You are likely to see time either in front of you, going left to right, or vice versa. Perhaps you see it as a "v", with you standing at the centre point, or the past coming from behind you, with the future stretched out in front of you.

If this hasn't helped fully, concentrate for a moment on your past memories and think of something that you do on a daily basis. It could be getting out of bed, taking a shower or cleaning your teeth.

Think of the time you did this yesterday, then last week, then six months ago. These past memories are forming a pattern. If you were to point to them, where would they be? What direction are they coming from? To your left or right, in front of you or behind you?

IN TIME/THROUGH TIME

What is the language you use about events in the past or future? Do you refer to, "putting things behind you", about unhappy or past events, or, "looking forward", to an event that's yet to happen?

If you're, "in time", you may well have pointed behind you, or to the rear side, or if any part of your time line moves through your body.

If you're, "through time", you're likely to have pointed in front of you or to the front left, if right-handed.

Now, go back to the daily task you used for establishing the past memory internally. See yourself showering or cleaning your teeth in the near future, tomorrow, next week, in 3 months time. What direction do these future thoughts come from? Point to them.

If it was pretty much directly in front, you're "in time".

If you're pointing to the front but out to one side, you're sorting, "through time".

Take your memory point in the past and your future memory point, as two points in the space around you somewhere. Now imagine a line connecting the two. This is your personal time line.

If it runs in front of you, like you're standing on the pavement with the road stretched out left to right, it's another indicator that you're, "through time".

If your time line runs through your body with your past behind you and the future in front, with you standing somewhere on it, or in it in the present, you're, "in time".

Most people fall into one category or another, or at the very least generally favour one definition from another.

Also, "through time", individuals tend to dissociate from their memories. That is to say they can see themselves in a past memory, as if watching, whereas, "in time", individuals see memories as if through their own eyes in an associated way.

I personally code, "through time". I like to be on time for meetings, don't enjoy being late, like structure, planning ahead and staying on track. A "lets get on now, or get this show on the road now" - a real urgency perspective.

If you're, "in time", you tend to have associated memories. You are more likely to be in the "moment", time has a different perspective. If you're a little late for a meeting, what the heck, it doesn't have the same effect on you as a "through time" person. Less planning perhaps, more of a, "take it as it comes" attitude, more flexible.

If you're "in time" you may well say things like, "put the past behind you", or, "you'll look back on this and laugh", whereas a "through time" person wouldn't say these things, as time is never behind them, it's always all in view for them.

All of this is useful to know because it can start to explain how a partner, friend or someone you are trying to establish rapport with has a different perspective on "Time" than you.

Let's take as an example a couple getting ready to go out for dinner. One is ready with time to spare whilst the other is in the moment, seeing no need to rush. The first is pushing because being late is not an option for them, whilst the other person feels that there is still plenty of time. This is because one of them is "through time", and the other "in time".

CREATE A FUTURE MEMORY OF SUCCESS

This is an exercise you can carry out on your own, but if you would like to work with a close friend you can both take it in turns to support each other. The goal does not have to be shared, unless you want to.

By physically walking your time line, the movement helps put memory into the muscle and create new neural pathways. It creates a sort of kinaesthetic "as if" frame. When actually going for your goal, your brain already has a positive memory encoded and is able to act "as if" you have done this before, thereby making attaining the goal familiar and therefore easier.

In preparation, follow these steps.

Step one.

Think of a goal you have set yourself, perhaps one from the goal setting action planner. It may be a goal set for the distant future or a goal that appears challenging, but it's compelling and you're really motivated to achieve it. Once you have decided the outcome you want specifically, i.e. what will I see, hear and feel, once I have it, move on to the next step.

Step two.

Imagine your time line on the floor. If you're on it that's fine, if it runs just in front of you step onto it. That's right, make yourself comfortable. You're on your time line now. Face towards the place that represents the future.

In a quiet environment, think about this brilliant goal in all its facets. What does it feel like and sound like? What are you hearing? Create a vivid internal representation of your goal and visualise it clearly. See yourself in this new memory.

There's no rush, take your time.

How will you know when you have achieved your goal? How is it going to make you feel inside once achieved? Picture the look on your face and anything else that will help you. See what you see through your own eyes. Make the picture bolder, brighter and even more compelling. When you're ready, move on to the next step.

Step three.

Choose a starting point for your goal (which may be right now). Put a marker down to mark the spot and walk forward keeping your end goal firmly in your mind. Walking into the future, along your personal time line, simply and steadily moving toward your goal, with each step bringing you closer to your goal, until you feel you are on the right spot to achieve it. We'll call this your "goal achievement point" - allow your unconscious to help you.

Step four

Now, as you stand in the future with your goal realised, look at your goal achievement point and see yourself achieving this goal as if seeing yourself in a movie or picture of the event. Think of a word that sums up this fantastic achievement for you and say it out loud.

Step five

Turn around on your time line and look back towards the start point at all the things you have done to achieve your goal and how all the steps have brought you here, taken one by one, but with unrelenting vision. You may like to write each step down. Each step took you closer to your goal achievement point. Take your time and notice what you notice. Be aware of all the little steps that made for this great result.

Now – Step six.

Time to leave your goal in the future, but connect it to the present.

Slowly turn back to face the future again and move gently backwards down your time line to your starting point. Don't look for it (you can just sense where it is this time), making a connection with the goal and the present, noticing what you notice and all the things you have done, all the steps you have taken to bring success.

As you travel back to the start point, from the achievement point, somehow link all the steps along the way. What would you choose to connect them? A rope, a chain, a golden thread weaved between them? Let you and your unconscious decide. Choose anything that helps, so that your future goal attainment success is linked to the start point and all the points in between.

Arriving back at the now, your starting point, you have a new awareness of all the steps that will take you on this compelling journey to success, your journey to achieving new goals. If you would like to step off your time line, (if through time), do whatever feels right.

Just take a moment to notice where your starting point was when you finished the exercise.

This process is a great way of getting support through extra insight from your unconscious, making really challenging goals become stepping stones to success.

TIME LINE EXERCISE

To further enhance the previous technique, draw your time line as a line on a clean sheet of paper. Your starting point is now and wherever you walked to becomes your achievement point for the goal you wanted to achieve, some point in the future.

As you examine the line you will remember your walk along it and the thoughts you were having, with every step you took. The energy, the emotions, the motivation, the fun.

Now draw some steps that link one end to the other, maybe stepping stones as circles or something else you choose.

Begin to list the actions that you need to take, the steps that will take you forward from today, moving you closer and closer to your goal. Allow your unconscious to work with your conscious thoughts, you may even like to close your eyes again if that will help.

Just let the thoughts work together, then having visualised the journey again and the steps you took, notice what you notice. Make a list of what actions would help you on this new and compelling adventure.

Now add each of the actions on your list to your time line, with the first step you plan to take, in the first stepping stone. Do the same with the rest. Start to take positive action. Remember, each step moves you closer to your goal.

Congratulate yourself with each and every success. Inspire others along the way.

MIND MAPPING

Mind mapping is another tool that can bring about greater clarity in achieving timed goals, as well as solving problems. It's not a new fad, it was actually developed in the 3rd century by a noted thinker Porphyry of Tyros.

It's a visual thinking tool that assists brainstorming, helps capture inspired thoughts and structures information, showing a way forward towards your chosen outcome.

For example, you may have a goal that you want to achieve but don't know where to start.

Take a clean sheet of paper and in the centre draw a circle or a square. It's your map, so you get to choose how it looks. You can then put a key word or symbol inside the shape, one that represents your goal.

Now, start to think about all the aspects of your goal, word or symbol you have chosen and draw lines coming out from the centre point, capturing every different thought, as a word or picture. Add colour if you like.

You will see how as one word or picture comes to you, another will lead off from it. Your map may well look like some branches or roots from a tree, going off in different directions, or become a colourful diagram with shapes and images.

This graphical way in capturing your thoughts utilises your creative right side of the brain and in doing so, gives you a new freedom and approach to solving a problem, or showing a clearer way forward.

The map which began with just one word or symbol has now become a strong focus representing your ideas and concepts in a creative new light, which can be used in many different situations. Using it to give further clarity to your time line's goals will bring the stepping stones closer together.

There is an example of a mind map in the Law Of Attraction chapter.

❖ FOOD FOR THOUGHT ❖

1. Time controls everyone's life. It's how effectively we use it that makes the difference.
2. Being more aware of how we experience time in our own minds, we can plan for future goals.
3. Most of us will experience the connection of past times and the future as a line.
4. Establish if you code time as "in time" or "through time", then walk your time line to a point where you can visualise the goal being achieved.
5. Use your time line to future pace aspirations and actions required to make your goals your reality.
6. Link each step taken in achieving you goal.
7. Enhance your positive memory imprint by carrying out the exercise of listing each success step between your start point and achievement point on your time line.
8. Mind maps allow our creative right side of the brain the freedom to create additional choices and captures inspired thoughts.

CHAPTER 7

THE LAW OF ATTRACTION

There are many laws that govern our universe, but none is more self-fulfilling than the law of attraction. The saying, "be careful what you think about, because it might just happen", came about as a direct result of the law of attraction.

This law is so incredibly powerful throughout the whole universe, that people who start to understand it and harness its energy can bring about amazing changes in their life. If this is the first time you have read about or been introduced to it, you will want to understand it more and more. Our thoughts really do control the lives we live.

POSITIVE VS NEGATIVE ENERGY

Every time we have a thought, it creates energy. Like a magnet, you will attract more of that into your life, but wait for it, this works with both good and bad. Therefore, positive energy and positive thoughts will bring about positive things.

We will concentrate on the positives, but just to help you understand the flip side and yourself a little better, do you remember a day when everything went wrong? The more frustrating the day became, the more wound up you were, the more things went wrong. It was as if everyone was conspiring against you, to see just how much crap you could put up with. Well guess what, the more focus you put on things going wrong and the more you thought negatively, the more grief you were given.

Your thoughts became your reality. The law states that like attracts like. So if you want to attract more good things into your life, have good thoughts and with good thoughts come good feelings.

I appreciate that you may be a little sceptical or unconvinced, there's a lot to take in. Remember the time when you were thinking about someone, a friend maybe and how nice it would be to give them a call. Just as you decided to walk over to the phone, it rang and at the other end of the line was your friend, who also had the same thought and at the same moment. Coincidence? Or could it really be that our thoughts have energy and can, and do travel?

Many authors, including highly respected coaches like Brian Tracy, have written about numerous laws that impact on our lives, and many others attribute their personal success and wealth to books including Think and Grow Rich. This was written in America back in the 1930's by Napoleon Hill, who throughout his book alludes to this law, having been in the privileged position of interviewing many of his country's top businessmen.

THE LAW IN ACTION

I have personally watched the law of attraction at work over many years, although for years I didn't understand how, and today I am still amazed at its awesome power. As a young chef about to get married, I had a good job, but had nowhere to live with my bride-to-be.

I must have been thinking of positive and creative ways to solve the issue, when something strange, yet magical happened. I was asked to go and work at a pub by a chef friend for a Saturday evening to help him out. In talking to the landlord following a successful evening in their restaurant, they then said that they were looking for a chef full-time as the business was growing and asked me if I was interested. I explained that I was soon to be married and was looking for a job with accommodation, to which they replied, "no problem, we have an empty cottage that you can have, if you take the job!"

The rest is history and although we moved on some months later to set up our own restaurant, (another great example of this law), the law of attraction had produced a home for us.

There are so many stories I could share with you that demonstrate the law of attraction and its amazing force, but the following is one of my favourites.

A young woman in her twenties told me this story, about a walk she was taking with her mum years earlier, when she was just 13. They were walking back from the village shops carrying their groceries, when the young girl looked up and saw a lad cycling past on a blue bike, that was far too small for him as his legs were going round really fast. She turned to her mum, who by now had also noticed this comical lad and proclaimed, "That's the boy I'm going to marry! He goes to my church."

The mum looked bemused and they carried on walking home. Many years later I heard this story from my wife Lin, who happened to be the girl in the story. What happened to the lad on the bike? She married him, it was me! We have been happily married for over 35 years, have two beautiful daughters and the law of attraction has happened in our lives time and time again.

The law of attraction isn't new. It's centuries old and has helped people build business empires, develop countries and create amazing masterpieces. People can attract a refreshing drink on a warm day, to a parking space in a busy mall, to a new home or a new career. So can you! If you're still thinking it's all down to luck, being in the right place at the right time, think again.

It is true, the roll of the dice will bring out a six at times, but having personally been upgraded on flights and given more luxurious hotel accommodation than I have purchased far more times than I can count, the law of attraction is ready to help if you believe and ask.

VISUALISE

In the chapter on visualisation, you will see how to visualise and I'll explain the power of a vision board. In the section on goal setting, there is a strategy for writing your life goals. Walking your time line, you can visualise your goals in the future being achieved and enjoy all the sensations that go with them. By coupling all that you are learning with the amazing law of attraction, the magnet effect will have the tremendous force of ensuring your goals become reality.

I have read story after story of individuals like you and I who have used the power of attraction to achieve their personal and business dreams. Goals can be achieved and surpassed, but you have to believe. Believe it can happen. Be open to inspired thoughts and take positive, confident action.

Concentrate on happy positive thoughts. Be grateful for all you have and all the good things that have already happened in your life. Be proud of who you are and what you stand for. Be generous in thoughts and deeds.

People have gone from rags to riches and from riches to great wealth, because they believed in this universal law and concentrated on what they wanted, rather than what they didn't want. You don't need to worry about the how, but do practise visualising when relaxed the outcomes you seek. These could be material or life enhancing, whether a new home or new relationship, the law can bring it about. When you have an inspired idea or thought, act on it!

GRATITUDE

Be grateful for what you have already. Some might say, "I'm broke and don't have a relationship", but they do have the eyes to read this message. You can feel the warmth of the sun on your back, see a beautiful sunset, or hear a kind gesture from a passer by.

As a contemporary artist, I have produced some coloured crystals made from fused glass. Every time I look at or hold it, I stand for a moment and as my old Gran used to say, count my blessings, all the things I am grateful for in my life. If I'm having a challenging day, it moves me instantly to a better place.

If you would like to find out more about these crystals, please feel free to take a look at my website – www.act4life.co.uk.

GRATITUDE EXERCISE

Make a list of all the things in your life you value and are grateful for. All the good things going on in your life and all the good things that have happened so far.

Now add to the list the things that would make your life more complete, more compelling, more satisfying. As with the list in goal setting, make positive statements along the lines of, "I am happy and thankful that...", or, "I am pleased and grateful that...".

Write them as if they were happening in your life right now. There are no right or wrong sentences as long as they are positive and realistic, you believe in them and they resonate with you.

Remember the lessons learnt in other chapters that the unconscious brain cannot tell the difference between real or imagined. By understanding this you can achieve the goals you set yourself. Once given the instruction by you, your unconscious will help start working to bring it about. Make your imagined goals your reality.

So, starting right now, focus on what you want in your life. If it's more income you need, you can attract it. A new career or better health, attract it. If it's a partner to share your life with, attract them to you!

LAW OF ATTRACTION MIND MAP

Create a law of attraction mind map. Chart all the possibilities this compelling and exciting knowledge of the law of attraction can bring into your life. If you haven't read the chapter on time lines yet, you will find helpful details on mind mapping there.

I have attached an example, to help inspire you, and your thoughts.

❖ FOOD FOR THOUGHT ❖

1. Every thought has a frequency and energy which controls the life we live.
2. Good thoughts create positive energy and good feelings.
3. Concentrate on happy, positive thoughts and be grateful for all you have.
4. Boost your goals using positive statements. Visualise success and believe.
5. Focus on what you want, rather than what you don't want in your life.
6. Visualise regularly when relaxed to attract good things into your life and be ready to act on inspired thoughts.

CHAPTER 8

VISUALISATION

With every page you are reading, you will have noticed a theme running throughout and linking each chapter, like a golden thread, one with another. Our thinking impacts on our lives, hour after hour, day after day, year after year. The images that you are holding in your mind now are as a direct result of your thoughts. You cannot see something without thinking about it. Likewise, you cannot hear something without trying to visualise it internally. Our thoughts are with us every moment of our waking hours and beyond.

If you are a total of your thoughts, by utilising a powerful and positive visualisation strategy, you can build an incredibly effective internal programme. This can not only help to ensure you give the best of yourself, but also get the best from your life.

VISUALISING AS CHILDREN

Visualisation might sound like a strange word, yet cast your mind and thoughts back to when you were young. Many of the games you played then and children play today, focused around visualisation. We copied what we saw others doing, then recalled it visually ourselves. From cops and robbers, doctors and nurses, to the tea party with pretend friends. We have played cowboys without Indians and become superheroes.

Our mum's old sheets became tents, our gardens became jungles with all sorts of prehistoric monsters lurking behind the bushes. Plasticine and Play-Doh have also played a great part in the imagination of children through them visualising, then creating a new pet or pretend character. Wallace and Gromit creator Nick Park recently recalled on television how he loved getting a new pack of plasticine for Christmas, so he could let his imagination run wild and start to create new models from his thoughts.

The phenomenally successful children's toy brick LEGO has shown that imagination and visualisation has helped to create fun over many years and there are billions of these little play bricks around the world and even theme parks made out of them.

THINK LARGE FLUFFY ANIMAL

If I was to say think of a large fluffy animal, you would make an internal representation of a large fluffy animal. The more detail I give you, for example, give it a friendly smile, fluffy yellow ears and big paws, the more it comes to life. You are now visualising clearly from your internal thoughts and recalling it from your vast memory bank of millions of pictures that you have stored. Even if I had asked you to visualise an animal you have never seen, you would have created a picture of what you think it might look like. This has all come about as a result of our map of the world, how we interpret it utilising our representational system, which I cover in chapter one.

Visualisation and imagination as a child has also played a key role in many of our careers. I'm sure if you think back to your childhood you will suddenly recall events that happened then, influencing you or even people you know today.

Let me give you an example. As a five year old, my older brother would regularly play at being a builder. I remember watching my uncle Steve loading a pretend wheelbarrow for him, then fully loaded with pretend sand and bricks my brother would set off across the room to the pretend site, pushing hard with all the weight, stopping along the way to get his breath back. Now, and for as long as I can remember he has been in the building industry and today works on some of the finest buildings in the country, with contracts running into many millions of pounds.

I want you to imagine how powerful the law of attraction could be if you turbocharged it with visualising the success, good health, contentment, happy relationships, in fact, whatever you want to enhance in your life.

REAL VS IMAGINED

Remember, another great piece of news is that our unconscious cannot differentiate between something that is real or imagined, so that gives us a fantastic canvas to paint the rest of our lives. Whatever we can think about, we can bring into our reality. We choose the colours, the brush and use as many ingredients as we like. Visualisation techniques are not new. Great artists from centuries ago were able to create masterpieces visually from what they saw in their minds.

The author and highly respected public speaker Dr Denis Waitley describes in the DVD, "The Secret", how he used the same visualisation programme on Olympic athletes that was used to train NASA astronauts in The Apollo space programme.

Visualisation techniques and research that has been done on many occasions, has constantly demonstrated that the unconscious mind cannot tell imagined from reality. Experiments carried out by him with the Olympic athletes included wiring them all up to sensors and then getting them to run the race in their minds from start to finish.

The results showed that the muscles of the runners fired in exactly the same sequence as they would have done had they run the race for real.

VISIONARIES

When you hear the term "Visionary", what thoughts does it conjure up? To me, it's about forward thinking individuals, thinking ahead, outside the box, with unwavering beliefs. Visualising how life and the future could be. It's not a term we hear that often, but behind every Visionary, is a Visualiser.

Thomas Edison, Isaac Newton, Mahatma Gandhi, Mother Teresa, Martin Luther King Jr and many, many others all had a vision and kept on visualising.

Scientists, peacemakers, politicians, businessmen like Henry Ford and many more incredibly talented individuals not mentioned here, all had one thing in common, the ability to visualise their thoughts, then harness them to good and positive effect.

Who do you think might be one of today's Visionaries? What lessons might we learn from them? There are lots more around than you might think, you only have to look.

You will also find that many business leaders and top athletes, sportsmen and women, even top salespeople, will visualise in detail a future event or presentation they are about to make and the successful outcome they are seeking. It works for them, as it can for you.

Visualising will also help show you what actions you need to take in preparation to reach your goals, which is also covered further in the Time chapter.

With this knowledge, we are able to apply it and use it effectively in our lives. By visualising the outcome of each goal we set ourselves, this mental preparation will help us to clarify that the goal we think we want to achieve, is exactly that, the place to focus our attention. Then the law of attraction will work with us to make it happen!

Each goal achieved has an impact on others around us, so this makes for a good reality check. Using visualisation as an ally, you will start to see how it can be harnessed in many situations-a forthcoming meeting, negotiation or conversation you are planning to have. Utilise role play, see yourself in the picture, visualise the outcome you would like.

Time spent in this way before important events in our life can be invaluable and enlightening. Your extra awareness makes you fully prepared, which in turn gives you more confidence and a far greater chance of the successful outcome you're seeking. Act "as if" you are in the conversation. Act as if you are a star in your chosen sport. Visualise goals as if you have already achieved them and learn from yourself the discoveries you make along the way.

A key to visualising is to do it in the present tense, as if it's happening now, feeling those good thoughts today, like a dress rehearsal before the first performance. Then mix your visualisation with belief, belief in yourself and believe it can happen. There's an old Latin proverb, "Believe that you have it, and you will have it."

Visualise what you do want and focus on the positives. In the book and DVD I have just mentioned, "The Secret", created by Rhonda Byrne, a chapter on the law of attraction says, anyone with financial worries visualising on debt, will get more debt, they will attract more of the same. Instead, visualise on prosperity and wealth, keep reframing your thoughts positively.

One of my personal heroes, a great visualiser, and another visionary, was a living legend during his life time, although sadly now longer with us, but is still talked about and influences millions of us today.

He too was a great thinker.

A man capable of great visualisation and imagination, so much so, that it would be hard for anyone around the world with young children not to have a toy or character somewhere about the home, evidencing his great imagination and creativity, nor an adult without one of his DVD's on the shelf.

Almost certainly, you will have been influenced by him or seen one of his films.

Walt Disney was able to dream and visualise so well that he has captured the imagination of millions of us, as well as moving our emotions. Think about any Disney film you have seen, as a child or adult and you will recognise that all our emotions come into play when watching them. Sad and worried one moment to triumphant the next. If Disney can move our emotions, so can we.

So you see from all of the above, that we already have it within us to visualise.

A few additional pointers which may help are first, to visualise from a relaxed, happy state. This will create the right emotional energy.

Many people also find closing their eyes to visualise a help.

Visualising takes practice, so do persevere.

VISION AND MOOD BOARDS

Many people have found that creating a visual focus for their goals and thoughts is not only fun, but creates an energy, clarity and more compelling motivation. When combined with the law of attraction and belief, vision and mood boards will bring great results, time after time after time.

You can use a board or a book to collect your goals, dreams and aspirations. Start by going through magazines and cutting out things that appeal to you. If you want to draw things, ideas or use words that are relevant, go ahead. For example, if your goal is to move home or buy your first house, start to find photos of a home you would enjoy living in. Cut out pictures of furniture that would go in your new home. Does it have a garden? How do you imagine the garden would look in the summer, in the winter? Pin everything you find on your board or place it in your book, but put them somewhere you will look at regularly, ideally every day. The clearer your thoughts, the clearer the details of the home become.

If you're creating a mood board to give you more happy emotions, cut out things that make you smile or feel good, things that resonate with you. Keep building the picture, utilise all your senses. What will you see, hear and feel when you have achieved this time in your life? What will it give you? What will it give others you care about?

I encourage my clients to think about colours too.

Start to visualise different colours and see how some make you feel good, whilst others create different emotions in you.

What colour would you choose that expresses fun or excitement?

What colour makes you feel calm and relaxed?

You could add these colours to your board.

Look at your board daily. Spend time being grateful for what you already have, allowing your thoughts to focus on where life's exciting journey is taking you. Believe, and don't be surprised as your goals and dreams become your reality. They have for many in the past and will for many in the future, including us.

If you would like to see some great examples of vision or mood boards, just search online for vision and mood boards at your next available opportunity, and you will see the creativity of others.

WAYS TO CREATE A HAPPIER STATE

We live as a result of our emotions and are always in one emotional state or another. The calmer we are, the easier we learn and the more resourceful we become. On the flip side, feeling angry or anxious can create a rollercoaster of frustration, disrupted thinking and poor judgement, because as the saying goes, we are not thinking straight. Think about the times people, who in a moment of anger or frustration, allow their emotional state to lose control, going on to say or do things they then live to regret, in some cases for the rest of their lives.

If you find yourself in a non-helpful or down state resulting in feelings of worry, anxiety or anger, you can break the unhelpful state quickly using one or any of the following that resonates with you.

Start by thinking of, then visualising someone smiling at you, someone who loves or really cares about you. Maybe carry a photo with you if this helps.

Do the breathing exercise of 4/4/4. Breathe in for 4 seconds, hold for 4 seconds and exhale for 4 seconds. Go through this exercise twice if you need to.

Change your physiology. If you're standing, sit down. If you're sitting, change position. Get up and go for a walk.

Go and talk to someone you respect.

For some, counting to ten does work, as it moves your thoughts to a new task.

Begin to think of all the positive, good things in your life. Think of 10 things that you are grateful for. Now think of another 10.

Try playing a piece of music you like, one that's associated with good, happy memories.

Watch a comedy or a programme that you're really interested in.

Think of something that made you really laugh, you know the time when you were laughing so much, you couldn't stop.

Use your heightened awareness to break unhelpful states before they spoil your day, or even your week. Your emotional state is in your control. You may not be able to control environmental influences, but you are in control internally. You get to chose how you respond to a situation.

Researchers tell us we have something like 60,000 thoughts a day, so it is natural that there will be times where you may feel you are going off track.

Knowing how to move into a better state when you're not in a good place, just by shifting your emotions using the sub-modality technique discussed in chapter one, or the technique I show you for relaxation, will help put you back on track fast..........along the road you want to follow.

❖ FOOD FOR THOUGHT ❖

1. Positive visualisation builds powerful internal motivational programmes.
2. By harnessing the law of attraction with visualisation, you can achieve great results.
3. Our unconscious cannot differentiate between real and imagined, so starts straight away at helping to bring about what we are visualising.
4. Create a vision or mood board to assist with your material and well-being goals.
5. Visualise in a happy, relaxed state. Do it regularly and persevere.
6. You have the personal internal resources to move yourself to a better place, when you need to. You get to chose how you respond to a situation.

If people like Walt Disney and Steven Spielberg can move our emotions, so can we.

CHAPTER 9

RELAXATION

If you spend your time constantly on the go, busy, with your mind jumping from one task to the next, formulating the next list of to do's, before catching your breath, you will find some helpful and useful strategies in this chapter.

If on the other hand, you're wondering why a book about thinking has anything to do with relaxation, you will discover how inextricably linked the two are.

What does the word relaxation or term chill out conjure up to you?

What do you do to relax?

If you have a pen handy, write down three or four things that come to mind. We will explore them later in the chapter.

Although being driven, focused and motivated are important to achieving our goals in life, by not maintaining a balance and taking time to relax and revalue situations, we may miss out on additional creativity and perspective that could make our lives easier. We may also miss out on other opportunities along the way, because, in the words of the saying, we can't see the wood for the trees. Moments of inspiration rarely come to us whilst under pressure or stressful tension.

Those who live life in the fast lane without relaxing are more susceptible to burnout, creating more problems for themselves, not least health related, than those who take time to relax or learn how to relax better.

I use the word learn, as for some this may become a journey of discovery.

WHAT IS RELAXATION?

So what is relaxation? What keys does it hold for our well-being and maxing out on a full and healthy life?

I believe relaxation offers relief from stress. For everyone though, it could be different. Some people can channel stress to great positive advantage and effect, whilst others feel stressed or uneasy with any form of change. Having a range of techniques that help us cope better with the pressures that unfold in our daily lives is essential.

Only this week, I was watching the news when it was announced that the British government were running a research programme for pregnant mums, teaching them relaxation and hypnotherapy techniques. It had already been established that mothers who were less anxious and stressed during childbirth suffered less pain through labour.

As I have previously said, we live our life in a range of different states. Being aware of how beneficial relaxation is and applying it as we go along life's journey, can be the difference between a life of pain and stress and one that brings fun and fulfilment.

Relaxation allows you to turn down the volume in your life sufficiently to hear yourself breathe, or take a few moments to be still and calm.

For others it may be to close their eyes and imagine a special place. The more we learn how to relax, the better we can function as human beings. Relaxation is good for us. With true relaxation, time stands still. Those who follow a sport or pursuit become so absorbed that hours can fly by. Listening to a favourite piece of music, watching a special film or chatting to friends can all have the same effect.

Many people I meet say they have little time to relax other than holidays. Being busy at work, then busy doing chores in the evening and at the weekend. We are on the go 24/7, with shops open 7 days a week and more sleepless nights. As a poem I recently read reminded me, we are so busy going about our lives, dashing from here to there, we often forget to enjoy the journey we are taking.

It's true that holidays can be relaxing and inspiring and a change of scenery or solitude can rejuvenate the soul and calm the mind, but living on the edge all year, tired, irritable and stressed, many go on holiday so fatigued that it takes most of the holiday to recover.

If any of the above resonates with you, there is so much that can be done to bring some calm and relaxation into your life.

Relaxation doesn't have to take hours either. I was talking with someone recently who told me that to sit and enjoy a coffee was their way of spending time relaxing, allowing themselves just to chill and be in the moment, a time to recharge their batteries.

LIST TO INSPIRE RELAXATION

I asked you earlier to write a list of what relaxation meant to you. Is any of what you have written on the list below? Can you add to it?

I have listed a number of different ways people use to relax. Go through the list and tick those that you have tried or activities you might like to try. All have the ability to reduce stress if approached correctly.

Anything that can move your thoughts from the everyday hustle and bustle, even if for a few minutes, can be invigorating and re-energise you, as they will bring about a different emotional state.

With each one on the following list you read, for example music, think of all the ways you could relax using this. It may be listening to a lovely piece of music, learning to play an instrument, joining a choir or singing, going to a karaoke event, maybe learning to rap or going to the opera. Music has so many possibilities to help you relax.

Think outside the box as you go through the list.

Taking exercise
Walking
Sport

Music
Hobbies
Meditation
Aromatherapy
Yoga
Thai chi
Phone a friend
Watch something funny. Cartoon/comedy.
Prayer
Change of scenery
Deep breathing exercises
Laugh
Read
Learn an interesting subject
Visit a place of peace
Visit a park/theme park
Visit a zoo
Visit a gym/spa
Take a relaxing bath
Enjoy a refreshing glass of water
Dance
Swim
Body massage
Head massage
Psychic massage
Visit a friend
Smile
Love someone
Watch a film
Cook a meal
Go out for dinner
Reflexology
Reiki

Crystal therapy
Hypnosis
Neuro-Linguistic Programming
Book a special event
Write a poem/story/book
Travel
Paint or draw
Do a puzzle
Do a crossword
Light a candle, then watch the dance of the flame
Gardening
Visualisation techniques
Religion
Use a coach
Coach yourself
List all the things in your life you're grateful for

This list is not exhaustive, add to it yourself. Some of the list may have made you smile, some not, but if it feels right or sounds good, give it a try. If you need to find out more about it, start looking now.

You may say some of the list relates to a task, sport or hobby, how will that help me relax? Remember that you start to relax when you move away from your conscious thoughts and any problems that are at the front of your mind, towards something that will bring balance and help you to put things in perspective.

Relaxing can also help bring inspired thoughts to personal challenges.

If you have already read the chapters on Law of Attraction or Visualisation, you will see how important the state of relaxation is to fully and effectively benefit from each of them.

Moving your state of mind need only take seconds. If you're feeling worried, anxious or in a stressful (or about to go into a stressful) situation, the quickest way to move your state is to do a breathing exercise, which can reduce your anxiety or fears in an instant.

BREATHING EXERCISES

This first technique takes just 12 seconds.

Breathe in for the count of four.
Hold your breath for four.
Now breathe out for four seconds.

Why not try it now? Experience how much more relaxed and calm you feel. When you consciously focus on your breathing, even for a brief time, it will bring you into this moment, the present. It's often said that our breath is the doorway to the now, as its happening right now.

There are many more breathing techniques taught in Yoga and meditation that you could explore. The following is just one example.

Start by just thinking about your breathing. As you take a breath in, put your hand on your tummy. Try to bring your breath all the way in and right down to your stomach, maybe even feel it moving your hand.

A long deep breath.

Imagine filling a clay pot with water. In the same way, use your in-breath to fill the bottom first (your stomach), then the middle (your ribs) and then the top (your chest).

Now breathe out. First exhaling the air from your chest...then your ribs...then from your tummy.

This three part breath is simple, yet totally effective.

Again, breathe in. First into your tummy...then your ribs, feeling them expand and then again into your chest. Now breathe out, first from your chest...then your ribs...then your stomach.

When your mind wanders, simply bring it back to your breath.

Do this exercise for as long as you find helpful, and practise. Its difficulty is in its simplicity.

JUST IMAGINE TECHNIQUE

Another useful technique that can also be done any time, but works best in a less noisy environment, is to think of a special place you have visited in the past. (You may find it helpful to read through this exercise first before doing it).

A place that is calm and tranquil, a place that holds special memories or it may even be a place you would like to visit and in visualising it, you can see yourself there, right now enjoying its peaceful surroundings.

Maybe it's a special beach, another country or a mountain range, a woodland or garden perhaps, but wherever this special place is, it brings you an inner peace and feeling of contentment.

As you picture this special place and if you're able to, close your eyes. Feel yourself relax, at peace with yourself and be in the moment. See yourself in the picture, seeing what you see, hearing what you hear and feeling what you feel.

Absorb yourself into this calm and special place and notice all the feelings and any colour that's associated with it. Is it warm or cool? Is there a breeze?

Can you hear sounds of water or birds singing in the background? Or is it so quiet you could hear a pin drop?

Hear each breath you take as you look around this special place, seeing yourself so clearly in the picture. Make the picture bolder and brighter and enjoy all the sensations that your body is absorbing in this special place.

That's right, relax and enjoy a few moments longer......and as you start to come back to the now of your life, open your eyes and feel totally awake. Notice how good and how relaxed you now feel, maybe even smiling in the knowledge that you can visit your special place whenever you like, you have lifetime admission!

❖ FOOD FOR THOUGHT ❖

1. Learning how to relax or relax better, keeps life's challenges in perspective and can make you feel great.
2. With full relaxation, time can stand still. Hours can pass as if minutes.
3. Anything that can move your thoughts away from stressful situations can help to recharge your batteries and put you in a more resourceful state.
4. Discover a new way to relax from the list, then think outside the box, then try it.
5. Using visualisation techniques without distraction can transport you to a safe, friendly and happy environment, anywhere in your world's imagination.
6. Explore other breathing exercises as a way of being in the moment.

CHAPTER 10

MORE FOOD FOR THOUGHT – INSPIRATIONAL QUOTES

Arriving at one goal is the starting point to another. John Dewey

Be modest, a lot was accomplished before you were born. Lou Holtz

It is not because things are difficult that we do not dare, it is because we do not dare, that they are difficult. Seneca

Nothing in life is to be feared, it is only to be understood. Marie Curie

Live as if you were to die tomorrow. Learn as if you were to live forever. Mahatma Gandhi

Aim high, live true. Alfred Tiffin

The healthiest response to life, is Joy. Deepak Chopra

Most people don't know what they are capable of. Roger Bannister

Nobody can make you feel inferior without your consent. Eleanor Roosevelt

Opportunity is nowhere, or now here! (Unknown)

People often say that motivation doesn't last. Well, neither does bathing – that's why we recommend it daily. Zig Ziglar

Our greatest battles are that with our own minds. Jameson Frank

I dream for a living. Steven Spielberg

Happiness, is when what you think, what you say, and what you do are in harmony. Mahatma Gandhi

The greatest glory in living, lies not in never falling, but in rising every time we fall. Nelson Mandela

For success, attitude is equally important as ability. Sir Walter Scott

If you are going through hell, keep going. Winston Churchill

He who is not courageous enough to take risks will accomplish nothing in life. Muhammad Ali

If you can't make a mistake, you can't make anything. Marva Collins

All our dreams can come true, if we have the courage to pursue them. Walt Disney

Whether you think you can, or whether you think you can't, you're right. Henry Ford

Many of the most precious, and beautiful gifts in life, money can't buy. Geoff Hart

I am a success today because I had a friend who believed in me, and I didn't have the heart to let him down. Abe Lincoln

If I had eight hours to chop down a tree, I'd spend six hours sharpening my axe. Abe Lincoln

Nothing can stop the man with the right mental attitude from achieving his goal. Nothing on earth can help a man with the wrong mental attitude. W W Ziege

It is hard to fail, but it is worse never to have tried to succeed. Theodore Roosevelt

Kites rise highest against the wind, not with it.
Winston Churchill

Know yourself and you will win all the battles. Sun Tzu

Leap and the net will appear. Julia Cameron

Faith is taking the first step, even when you don't see the whole staircase. Martin Luther King, Jr

For our own success to be real, it must contribute to the success of others. Eleanor Roosevelt

I find that the harder I work, the more luck I seem to have. Thomas Jefferson

Age is a number...not a disability. Lin Hart

Life is like a coin, you can spend it any way you wish. But you only spend it once. Lillian Dickson

Treat people as if they were what they ought to be, and you will help them become what they are capable of becoming. J W Von Goethe

Happiness is related to the way we think. If we do not train our minds, and do not reflect on life, it is impossible to find happiness. Dalai Lama

We make a living by what we get. We make a life by what we give. Winston Churchill

Personality opens the door, but character keeps the door open. Sir Alan Sugar

Most folks are about as happy as they make up their minds to be. Abe Lincoln

Act "as if" you are all the things that you aspire to be. Clare Collins

The purpose of life, is a life of purpose. Richard Byrne

There's no such thing as work life balance. When you think about it, it's all life. Richard Branson

INSPIRED THINKING/YOUR QUOTES

As you go through the list of quotes, I guess a few may have struck a chord with you.

Some are inspiring, others motivational, but all give an insight into the way the contributor thinks and in some cases live, or sum up their philosophies on their own journeys through life.

Quotes are great because they make us think.

They can start a train of thought that moves us, but quotes are not just for the rich and famous and you have as much right as anyone else on the planet to come up with quotes of your own.

Maybe not today, maybe not tomorrow, but sometime soon, you will say something that is motivational or inspiring to you and could be to others.

Enjoy the creativity. Don't forget it. Write it down straight away and if you would like to send me your quote, I will do all I can to publish it in my next book. You're welcome to stay in touch by emailing.........info@act4life.co.uk

There are some wonderful quotes around the world and if you enjoyed looking at the few enclosed over the past pages, take some time to look for others.

Why not keep your own journal of quotes that you find helpful or inspire you into action with your life goals? Pin a couple up on your vision board or on a fridge or office wall, to remind and keep you motivated.

You won't have to look very far either. There are some great books full of quotes and thousands on the web. We can all learn from others and be motivated by them, especially people we admire or respect, even from a distance.

"If you can dream it, you can do it." Walt Disney

CHAPTER 11

SOME FINAL THOUGHTS

As you have seen through each chapter, your thoughts have a direct impact on your health, well-being, confidence, success and every goal you set yourself during your lifetime.

That makes for a lot of thinking and the better focused you are on what's really important to you, the more fulfilled and at peace with yourself you will become. I hope this book, with its different tools and exercises, goes some way to showing you that whatever your challenges, whatever you want to achieve in your life, by taking positive actions, by coaching your thoughts, your hopes and aspirations can become your reality.

Throughout the book you have explored some NLP techniques with your unique maps of the world. These techniques will enable you to build a more compelling and rewarding future. Within these final thoughts, I will also answer some additional questions which may also be useful to you.

MORE ABOUT NEURO-LINGUISTIC PROGRAMMING

Neuro-Linguistic Programming, a totally safe and holistic process, came about by research undertaken by Richard Bandler a mathematics student, and John Grinder, a professor of linguistics in the 1970's. In essence, they developed a series of identifiable processes or techniques that have enabled others to be exceptional, and can be taught to you and I.

They modelled the language, thought processes state, unconscious and conscious behaviour and techniques of the leading individuals in the field of therapy in America at the time. Namely, hypnotherapist and psychotherapist Milton Erickson, family therapist Virginia Satir and Gestalt therapist Fritz Perls, who Richard spent time with whilst he was working with the publisher of Fritz's books.

These two young pioneers identified the key points that all three therapists had in common, and studied the difference between the ordinary results and the outstanding results. They then set about analysing and distilling all the information they had gathered into a number of repeatable processes (techniques) that others could easily learn and utilize, to achieve outstanding, and magical results too.

Then they began to apply the same modelling techniques, in a number of different fields such as communication, business and sport, and through their diligence they developed a sort of human excellence software for the brain.

As a result of utilising this human excellence software for the brain, we can experience more peak performance in our lives, form better relationships, achieve goals, utilise self-motivation and enjoy a more positive outlook, as well as banishing phobias quickly and effectively.

As you will have discovered by utilising the numerous techniques contained in this book, this reprogramming software allows you to have the kind of experiences you want, and to handle situations in an effective way, without compromising your own values.

NLP PRE-SUPPOSITIONS

We make pre-suppositions all the time in our everyday lives. Earlier in the book, I introduced you to some of the NLP pre-suppositions, ones including "You cannot, not communicate".

These pre-suppositions form the basis of success of NLP. They are also used as principles of conduct. This chapter enables me to expand on this further, and introduce a few more to you, as they can help to shift your thinking fast, and take you from a mind set like concrete, to one with more flexible possibilities and options.

In the NLP workbook by Joseph O'Connor, he describes pre-suppositions as its guiding philosophy. These principles are not claimed to be true or universal. You do not have to believe that they are true. But because you pre-suppose them to be true, then act as if they were, they form a set of ethical principles for life.

1) Every behaviour has a positive intention.

I am sure this statement may have raised a few eyebrows, so to further explain, NLP separates out the positive intention from the behaviour, so that we can also separate the person from the behaviour, and know that a person is not their behaviour.

Even though a particular behaviour may be interpreted as negative, the intention behind it is a positive one for the person carrying it out. When a person has a better choice of behaviour that can also achieve their positive intention, they will take it.

NLP cannot change a person's experience, but it can enable a person to change their belief about, response to and perception of that experience...and therefore to change their behaviour.

2) Modelling successful performance leads to excellence.

You will find many progressive companies where successful managers, salespeople and skilled employees are modelled. Many coaches are employed to go and work with such individuals, watch them and talk to them, learn to understand how they work and then use this new knowledge to assist others achieve a more effective result in their chosen field. This behavioural modelling has been applied over a wide range of contexts, including in the workplace and in personal relationships, and has produced techniques that will also enable you to take yourself to a new level of success.

Just think of someone who showed or taught you a great technique, it could be in sport, a hobby or anything else. Once you had practised and mastered it, you took yourself to a new level of success. So it is with life.

3) People make the best choice they can at the time.

Sometimes clients I see have been reflecting on, then agonising over past decisions, leading them to feel guilty, upset or frustrated. This pre-supposition confirms that the best decision was made from the information and resources available at that time. Now is the time to let go of these feelings on past decisions and take any learning from them. Realise that the better the map of the world you can build for the future, the better the choices you will make from the options, as well as having more flexibility.

4) If you want to understand, act.

The learning is in the doing. Throughout the book there have been many tools and exercises as well as numerous NLP techniques. To get the most from them, act....ion is required.

Action will bring new learning, new understanding, new promise.

It's the same with the Law of attrACTION. You can see how action is key to bringing this law into fruition, and it's the same for setting goals. It's also why my coaching business is called act4life.

One final thought regarding act, which I know I have covered earlier, but it is worthy of repeating. If you act "as if", you are all the things you aspire to be, you are already on your way.

If you want promotion in the workplace, act as if you have the new responsibility. This heightened awareness, this enthusiasm and commitment will get noticed and when the opportunity unveils itself, you will have put yourself in the best possible place.

MY PERSONAL MESSAGE

My wish for you is that by reading this book, you have gained new resources, and uncovered yet more hidden talent that you didn't know, or forgotten you had, and in some way you have been inspired to take positive action.

Action to explore new compelling possibilities or take new confident steps to find answers you're seeking, and as you continue your journey of self-development, attract inspired actions to assist and expand your understanding, as well as your knowledge in areas that interest you, or you're just plain curious about.

As the saying goes, life is a journey, not a destination.

So as you continue on your journey, give yourself even more precious memories by allowing your unconscious to work alongside as a creative, intuitive support. Grow to like yourself more and more, and be proud of your reflection.

Being coached or coaching yourself enables us all to find a way forward. A way that can work for us as individuals, to seek our own answers, to trust our internal resource, tap into our unconscious thoughts, and use the models that have worked for, and helped others.

I'm still learning. I still use these tools myself, but I am committed to making every day count and to improving my life, and the contribution I make. I take time to reflect on, and be grateful for things that I could so often take for granted. A sunny day, a beautiful sunset and the love of a family.

The challenges of our life don't go away, we just learn new ways to improve our mental state quickly and effectively. Remember, no one can make you angry, frustrated or hacked-off without your consent. You choose.

I have really enjoyed writing this book, which I hope has provided some of the answers you were seeking, and given you deeper understanding as you continue on your journey through life.

This book's journey has given me an opportunity to reflect, and in doing so I have learnt even more about myself, so thank you.

I sincerely wish you well, and look forward to hearing your success stories as they unfold, along with any food for thought you might like to share. Stay in touch at..... info@act4life.co.uk

To conclude I leave you with a few more thoughts from Mother Teresa.

Warm regards,

Geoff

MOTHER TERESA – LIFE

Life is an opportunity, benefit from it.
Life is beauty, admire it.
Life is bliss, taste it.
Life is a dream, realize it.
Life is a challenge, meet it.
Life is a duty, complete it.
Life is a game, play it.
Life is a promise, fulfil it.
Life is sorrow, overcome it.
Life is a song, sing it.
Life is a struggle, accept it.
Life is a tragedy, confront it.
Life is an adventure, dare it.
Life is luck, make it.
Life is too precious, do not destroy it.
Life is life, fight for it.

Mother Teresa

ACKNOWLEDGEMENTS

Over the years, I have learned from and been influenced and inspired by many individuals.

Some, like Brian Tracy, Richard Bandler, John Grinder, Rhonda Byrne, Dr Denis Waitley, and the late Walt Disney, I have already mentioned within the book, and to whom I owe a deep gratitude.

The Coaching Academy Group, (recently becoming the world's largest Coach Training Organisation) for setting me on a fulfilling journey, and for bringing renewed purpose and motivation. With personal thanks to all the great trainers, and in particular NLP Coaches Ann Skidmore and Sarah Urquhart.

This page also gives me an opportunity to mention and publicly thank the following friends, family, and clients.

First, some of my coaching clients, without whom I would not have received such valuable input and feedback:

Justin, Paul, Cath, Phil, Steve, Nick, John, Clare, Nicky, David, Lucas, Sarah, and with special thanks to Alison.

Illustrator Ian Long for his help in adding humour and bringing his Blob cartoons to life. Ian's work with Pip

Wilson, creator of the highly regarded Blob Tree, is used by many counsellors to help people, particularly youngsters overcome personal challenges.

My wife Lin for her love, understanding, and patience as I embarked upon the journey to write The Thought Coach.

A very special thanks to Pat Mason of Shen-Dao Therapies in Oxford, who helped select, and review each of the NLP strategies, working with me to ensure they had a real clarity and would allow maximum positive results, and outcomes for each reader.

Son-in-law Paul, for his thought provoking questions to my script as he proof read and helped edit each chapter, encouraging me to expand where necessary, and give further lucidity to each model and exercise.

My long term friend, Phil Nightingale for inspiring and encouraging me to concentrate on my coaching skills, develop them further, and fulfil my mission in helping others.

My coaching buddies Clare Collins from Plan, and John Hardwick of Morefrom coaching, both of whom have continued to coach, support and motivate me over the past years.

John La Valle from "NLP Seminars Group International" for clarifying points, and taking the time to exchange emails, whilst busy travelling the USA presenting seminars with Richard Bandler and Kathleen La Valle.

Not least, to all those whose quotes or research may have inspired "new thinking" in you.

Just as importantly, to you, the reader, my sincerest gratitude and thanks.

CAPTURE YOUR THOUGHTS

CAPTURE YOUR THOUGHTS